Managing Uncertainty in the
House of Representatives

Managing Uncertainty in the House of Representatives

Adaptation and Innovation in Special Rules

Stanley Bach
Steven S. Smith

THE BROOKINGS INSTITUTION
WASHINGTON, D.C.

Copyright © 1988 by

THE BROOKINGS INSTITUTION

1775 Massachusetts Avenue, N.W., Washington, D.C. 20036

Library of Congress Cataloging-in-Publication Data

Bach, Stanley.
  Managing uncertainty in the House of Representatives.
  Includes index. 1. United States. Congress. House. Committee on
Rules—History. 2. United States. Congress. House—Rules and
practice—History. 3. Legislation—United States—History.
I. Smith, Steven S., 1953–
II. Title.
KF4997.R8B33   1988   328.73'05   88-30424
ISBN 0-8157-0742-8 (alk. paper)
ISBN 0-8157-0741-X (pbk. : alk. paper)

9 8 7 6 5 4 3 2 1

Set in Linotron Caslon 540
Composition by Graphic Composition, Inc.
Athens, Georgia
Printing by R.R. Donnelley and Sons, Co.
Harrisonburg, Virginia
Book design by Ken Sabol

In memory of
Charlotte Bach
and
Michael Smith

Foreword

EVEN the most casual observer of Congress recognizes that the House of Representatives has changed in fundamental ways since the early 1960s. A more assertive membership, expanded staffs, a decentralized committee system, reinvigorated party caucuses, and the new budget process were among the developments that altered the operations of the House and the dynamics of legislative policymaking during the 1970s. These changes have become well known. What is less well recognized is how different the House of the 1980s is from the House of the 1970s.

Stanley Bach and Steven S. Smith explore a key ingredient of House procedures and politics in the 1980s and beyond: the use of restrictive special rules. A special rule is a resolution the House adopts to consider a particular bill or resolution and to structure the debate and amending process affecting that measure. For more than a century, these resolutions have been a critically important device of the majority party leadership for setting the agenda of the House. During the last decade, the House's Democratic leaders and its Committee on Rules have used special rules in innovative ways, provoking repeated controversy, particularly among members of the Republican minority, who argue that many rules unfairly limit their opportunities to amend legislation on the floor. The authors provide the first comprehensive and dispassionate look at the developments in special rules since the mid-1970s. They examine the circumstances that led to innovations in special rules, the changing frequencies and patterns of their provisions, reactions among representatives to these developments, and the consequences of such procedural innovations for House politics and policymaking.

Stanley Bach is a specialist in the legislative process at the Congressional Research Service of the Library of Congress. Steven S. Smith, a former senior fellow in the Brookings Governmental Studies program, is associate professor of political science at the University of Minnesota. The authors wish to express their appreciation to Robert E. Bauman, Richard Bolling, John J. Dooling, Janet Hook, Keith Krehbiel, Thomas

E. Mann, Bruce I. Oppenheimer, Barbara Sinclair, Kristi Walseth, Ari Weiss, and Donald R. Wolfensberger for sharing their experiences, insights, and advice. They also are indebted to the representatives and the other House staff members who contributed their perspectives on developments in House politics and procedures. Nancy Davidson provided editorial advice on style and content, and Forrest A. Maltzman, Morton P. Soerensen, and Thomas J. Weko contributed research assistance. Shirley Kessel prepared the index, Peter Dombrowski verified the factual content, and Susan L. Woollen prepared the manuscript for typesetting. The authors thank Sandra Z. Riegler and Eloise C. Stinger for their administrative support and Renuka D. Deonarain for secretarial assistance. In addition, Stanley Bach happily acknowledges his debt of gratitude to his present and former colleagues at the Congressional Research Service, and to the members and staff who have contributed to his understanding of the legislative process.

The interpretations and conclusions presented in this book are those of the authors and should not be ascribed to any of the persons or organizations acknowledged above, including the Congressional Research Service, or to the trustees, officers, or staff members of the Brookings Institution.

BRUCE K. MACLAURY
President

September 1988
Washington, D.C.

Contents

Tables

CHAPTER ONE

The Rules Committee
in the House

WHEN THE House of Representatives convened on May 26, 1988, its members looked forward to a calm but productive day. It was to be the last meeting of the House before the week-long Memorial Day recess, and representatives knew they would be voting that day on the final version of Congress's budget plan for the coming fiscal year. Throughout the Reagan presidency, these budget resolutions had been highly contentious, provoking disagreements and sometimes pitched battles between Congress and the president, the House and the Senate, and congressional Democrats and Republicans. But not in 1988. The "budget summit" agreement of late 1987 between the president's men and congressional leaders of both parties, as well as the prospect of the 1988 elections, had taken the steam out of budgetary politics for the year. Although it had taken House and Senate negotiators longer than expected to reach a final agreement, there was no doubt that the House would approve their conference report. And although members could expect the final vote to be relatively close, they anticipated that the debate itself would be unusually brief and without the passion and vituperation of years past. So representatives would be able to return home with the budget deficit safely behind them as a political issue until after the November election.

The other legislative business of the day, passing a bill authorizing funds for intelligence activities, also promised to be routine. Almost as soon as the Speaker called the House to order at 10:00 A.M., the members promptly approved the resolution, commonly known as a "special rule," by which the House agreed to consider H.R. 4387, the intelligence bill. This resolution, which had been proposed by the House Committee on Rules, also contained certain ground rules for debating and amending the bill. Then, as debate began on H.R. 4387 itself, the chairman of the Permanent Select Committee on Intelligence, Louis Stokes of Ohio, and his Republican counterpart, Henry Hyde of Illinois, engaged in the kind

1

of mutual congratulations that usually presage smooth passage for bills across the House floor.

Stokes concluded his opening statement on the bill by paying tribute to Hyde for "his thoughtful and cooperative approach," and to Richard Cheney of Wyoming, the ranking Republican on the Subcommittee on Program and Budget Authorization, for working "tirelessly and effectively" to develop the bill. For their parts, Hyde and Cheney expressed support for the measure and took time to honor Stokes, who was completing his last year as chairman of the Intelligence Committee. Cheney complimented his chairman for his fairness, even while observing that "on many of the issues of the day we have fundamentally different approaches, and I am not one who often sings the praises of the leadership of my colleagues on the other side of the aisle." And Hyde's praise would deserve a place of honor in any collection of rhetorical flourishes heard on Capitol Hill: "There is a line in Camelot where King Arthur says all of us are tiny drops in a vast ocean, but some of them sparkle. Even though we have struggled and fought over issues and will again shortly, I just want to say Lou Stokes is one of the sparklers."[1]

With no storm clouds in sight, Stokes decided that the House need not engage in the plodding process of opening the bill to floor amendments one title at a time. Members approved the committee's own amendment to the bill without any debate at all and quickly adopted another amendment with bipartisan support. But then something unusual happened, something that disturbed the calm and good feeling on the floor for the next three hours. Hyde and Cheney broke one of the House's unwritten rules by proposing a controversial amendment without first informing Stokes, whom they had just praised so warmly. It is considered bad form to "blindside" a committee chairman in this way; it also is inconsistent with a conception of the House as a forum for making policy decisions on their merits. And it usually is bad politics as well. Springing an amendment on an unsuspecting chairman almost certainly guarantees that he will oppose it, and committee chairmen win on the House floor far more often than they lose.

In fact, Cheney began his defense of their amendment by "apologizing to my colleagues for the fact that we have had to bring this amendment up without the kind of notice we would ordinarily hope to be able to exchange," and Hyde later apologized as well, asserting that there had been "nothing more painful in my congressional career than not notifying

---

1. *Congressional Record*, daily edition (May 26, 1988), pp. H3654–56.

the gentleman from Ohio . . . of the amendment. . . ."[2] Why then did these two senior and well-respected Republicans decide it was necessary to violate one of the House's most widely accepted norms of comity? Because, they argued, they had no choice; if they had not offered their amendment by surprise, they would not have been able to offer it at all, or so they feared.

The amendment Hyde presented sought to eliminate restrictions on the use of funds by the Central Intelligence Agency, the Defense Department, or other agencies of government to support military or paramilitary operations in Nicaragua in support of the contras. Thus he and his colleague once again were raising one of the most controversial issues to bedevil the House during the 1980s. The position of the House had seesawed over the past several years, and advocates of military aid now were looking for an opportunity to force yet another floor vote on the issue. H.R. 4387 gave them their chance, but only if the House did not approve a special rule for the bill that restricted the floor amendments that members could offer and so prevent them from proposing their contra aid amendment. That is precisely the danger they had anticipated, and the reason they decided not to notify the Democratic leadership of their plans. Cheney explained:

> The difficulty we have encountered on this side [of the political aisle] in being able to offer amendments, the growth in restrictive rules that allow no amendments to bills, led us to believe that if we did in fact surface in advance today our intention to have a debate on Nicaragua and the situation there, that we would not be allowed to do so by the leadership of the majority party.[3]

So it was to avoid being foreclosed by a restrictive special rule for considering the intelligence bill that Hyde and Cheney decided they would have to offer their amendment without any advance warning. Although their amendment ultimately was rejected, 190–214, at least they had their debate and their vote, even if it meant ratcheting still higher the level of mutual suspicion and distrust in an already polarized House.[4]

2. Ibid., pp. H3666, H3670. See also Don Phillips and Joe Pichirallo, "House Republicans Jolt Democrats on Contra Aid," *Washington Post*, May 27, 1988, p. A26.

3. *Congressional Record*, daily edition (May 26, 1988), p. H3666.

4. Responding to Cheney's explanation, Democrat Matthew McHugh of New York suggested that the tactics the two Republicans had adopted might be self-defeating in the long run: "I would also say that if the minority fears that the leadership will craft restrictive rules

Cheney was not alone in his assessment of what was happening in the House. Just two days earlier, he and other Republicans had taken to the House floor for more than an hour to criticize the performance and practices of the House, including (but by no means limited to) what Trent Lott of the Rules Committee characterized as "the increasing reliance on so-called restrictive rules which limit the right of Members to offer amendments." "Oh, we're told gag rules are needed for time management and efficiency," exclaimed Lott, who also was the Republican whip, "but that's really a euphemism for political expediency." [5]

In late April the Rules Committee had reported precisely the kind of resolution to which Republicans were objecting. At issue was a bill, H.R. 4222, to extend the period during which undocumented aliens could apply for legalization under the landmark immigration law of 1986. The rule proposed that only two members be allowed to offer one amendment apiece; the other 433 representatives would have no such opportunity. [6] Yet the minority hardly could complain that it was being "gagged"; the two amendments were to be proposed by Republicans, not Democrats. And in fact, there were no Republican outcries of "political expediency." During the brief debate, the only criticism of the rule was a passing half-hearted comment by one of the two Republicans whose amendments were protected. Another Republican, Dan Lungren of California, explained why the rule was fair: "The accommodations have been made, and the members of the minority who wish to amend the bill before us will be given that opportunity." [7] The House then approved the rule so quietly and peacefully that most members undoubtedly were unaware of what had happened.

These two incidents will pass unnoticed when the history of the 100th Congress eventually is written. But they illustrate the subject of this book, which is an important and controversial development affecting how the contemporary House of Representatives does its business: the changing part the House Rules Committee has come to play in the legislative process as it drafts the resolutions, or special rules, that govern consider-

---

in the future, they are playing into the hands of the leadership. Many of us on the majority side believe that the minority should have an opportunity to offer serious amendments such as this, but we also believe that notice is important in fairness to the Members of the House, and therefore if the minority withholds reasonable notice on significant amendments I will urge the leadership to craft restrictive rules." Ibid., p. H3670.

5. Ibid. (May 24, 1988), p. H3578. For the Democratic response, see ibid. (June 9, 1988), pp. H4098–4107. See also David S. Broder, "How About a Little Glasnost for the House?" *Washington Post*, May 29, 1988, p. C7.

6. *Congressional Record*, daily edition (April 21, 1988), pp. H2175–78.

7. Ibid., p. H2177.

ation of major legislation on the House floor. What conditions and trends led to the ways in which the House considered the intelligence and immigration bills in the spring of 1988? Why have a majority of representatives so often voted to prohibit themselves and their colleagues from offering floor amendments that satisfy the normal requirements of the House's rules? What forms have these restrictions taken, and under what circumstances have they been imposed? How has this development affected the relations between the two parties and among the House's members, their standing committees, and their party leaders? These are among the questions we shall address.

Ever since the days of Speaker Reed in the 1890s, the House Rules Committee and its decisions have been critically important to the strategies of House party leaders and committee chairmen.[8] What has changed from time to time are the ways in which, and the purposes for which, the committee has exercised its powers. In the chapters to follow, we shall be analyzing how the committee has adapted to recent changes in the House, and some of the consequences that followed in their wake, through innovations in the provisions of special rules. As the title of this book suggests, we shall argue that several of the "reforms" the House adopted were among developments that caused significant uncertainties in the House. In response, we shall conclude, the Rules Committee has sought to manage these uncertainties in ways that, in different respects and to different degrees, have served the interests of standing committees, majority party leaders, and representatives generally.

The many changes that took place in the House during the early and mid-1970s combined to produce a much less stable, predictable environment for the Rules Committee and for everyone else in the House.[9] New issues and new members disrupted old ways of doing business, while a variety of organizational and procedural reforms redistributed influence and resources in ways that were not always anticipated. The Rules Committee, confronted with altered conditions and changing demands,

8. For additional information and background on the Rules Committee, see, for example, Bruce J. Dierenfield, *Keeper of the Rules: Congressman Howard W. Smith of Virginia* (University Press of Virginia, 1987); Spark M. Matsunaga and Ping Chen, *Rulemakers of the House* (University of Illinois Press, 1976); Bruce I. Oppenheimer, "The Rules Committee: New Arm of Leadership in a Decentralized House," in Lawrence C. Dodd and Bruce I. Oppenheimer, eds., *Congress Reconsidered* (Praeger, 1977), pp. 96–116; James A. Robinson, *The House Rules Committee* (Indianapolis: Bobbs-Merrill, 1963); and *A History of the Committee on Rules*, Committee Print, House Committee on Rules, 97 Cong. 2 sess. (Government Printing Office, 1983). The last of these sources also includes a useful bibliography.

9. See Barbara Sinclair, *Majority Leadership in the U.S. House* (Johns Hopkins University Press, 1983), pp. 1–29.

reacted by devising new strategies that have been embodied in the special rules it has reported. In brief, these rules have become more complex
in their form and varied in their provisions but also more likely to be
restrictive in their effect on amending activity. The result has been to
entangle legislative policy with procedure in innovative and intricate
ways, as the Rules Committee and Democratic party and committee leaders have sought ways to manage uncertainty in the postreform House.

An Overview of the Process

Most controversial bills and resolutions must receive special rules if they
are to reach the House floor for debate, amendment, and passage. When
one or more House committees report a measure and recommend that the
House consider and pass it, that bill or resolution is placed on one of
several "calendars," which essentially are catalogs of legislation eligible
for floor consideration. But there is no guarantee that all the legislation
on these calendars actually will reach the floor. To be taken from its place
on a calendar and called up on the floor, a measure must be "privileged"—meaning that it may interrupt the daily order of business laid out
in the House's standing rules.[10] A few classes of legislation, such as budget resolutions and general appropriations bills, enjoy this privilege, but
most measures do not. For the vast majority of bills and resolutions,
which are not privileged, there are three primary routes to the House
floor. First, a measure can be considered by unanimous consent, but only
if no member of the House objects. Second, it can be passed under a
motion to suspend the rules, but only if the Speaker agrees and two-thirds
of the members vote for it. Third, and most realistically for important
legislation, it can be considered and passed by simple majority vote under
the terms of a special rule.

To this end, the Rules Committee reports House resolutions that typically begin by proposing to make a particular bill or resolution in order
for floor consideration (see figure). In addition, each of these special
rules, or simply "rules," normally recommends a package of conditions

10. Rule XXIV, clause 1, in *Constitution, Jefferson's Manual and Rules of the House of Rep-
resentatives of the United States*, H. Doc. 99–279, 100 Cong. 1 sess. (GPO, 1987), pp. 627–29.
(Hereafter *House Rules and Manual*.) For a general discussion of this subject, see Walter J.
Oleszek, *Congressional Procedures and the Policy Process*, 2d ed. (Washington, D.C.: CQ Press,
1984), pp. 99–123; and Stanley Bach, "Arranging the Legislative Agenda of the House of
Representatives: The Impact of Legislative Rules and Practices," report 86-110 GOV
(Congressional Research Service, June 1, 1986).

House Calendar No. 31

100TH CONGRESS
1ST SESSION

H. RES. 183

[Report No. 100–119]

IN THE HOUSE OF REPRESENTATIVES

JUNE 2, 1987

Mr. GORDON, from the Committee on Rules, reported the following resolution;
which was referred to the House Calendar and ordered to be printed

---

RESOLUTION

Providing for the consideration of the bill (H.R. 2330) to authorize appropriations to the National Science Foundation for the fiscal year 1988, and for other purposes.

Resolved, That at any time after the adoption of this resolution the Speaker may, pursuant to clause 1(b) of rule XXIII, declare the House resolved into the Committee of the Whole House on the State of the Union for the consideration of the bill (H.R. 2330) to authorize appropriations to the National Science Foundation for the fiscal year 1988, and for other purposes, and the first reading of the bill shall be dispensed with. After general debate, which shall be confined to the bill and which shall not exceed one hour, to be equally divided and controlled by the chairman and ranking minority member of the Committee on Science, Space, and Technology, the bill shall be considered for amendment under the five-minute rule. At the conclusion of the consideration of the bill for amendment, the Committee shall rise and report the bill to the House with such amendments as may have been adopted, and the previous question shall be considered as ordered on the bill and amendments thereto to final passage without intervening motion except one motion to recommit.

and procedures to govern action on that measure, especially the amendments to it which members may propose. The House then debates the merits of the resolution, which itself is privileged for consideration, and agrees to it or rejects it by simple majority vote.[11] Once the House adopts the rule for a measure, it then can consider it under whatever terms the rule provides. The responsibility for designing and recommending these special rules inevitably puts the Rules Committee at the juncture of the House's standing committees, the majority party leadership, and the members of the House acting individually and collectively on the floor. Consequently, the committee's location in the legislative process makes it an excellent vantage point from which to examine the consequences of institutional and political change in the House.

During recent years, the Democratic majority on the Rules Committee has been drawn into a close working relationship with the Speaker and the caucus of all House Democrats, but this was not always the case.[12] Especially during the 1950s, when the Republican members on Rules would join forces with several conservative Democratic colleagues, including the committee's chairman, to form a conservative coalition, Rules was criticized for sometimes refusing to grant the rules necessary for liberal bills to reach the floor or go to conference.[13] The ultimate result was the dramatic 1961 struggle to add three new members to the committee in an attempt to give it a more dependable Democratic majority. In the next chapter, we shall touch on other changes in the committee's membership and its relations with the Speaker and the Democratic Caucus. At the moment, however, we need only emphasize that when members criticize the Rules Committee today, it is rarely because of its failure to grant rules. Instead, controversy is much more likely to surround the provisions of the rules it does report, especially the provisions affecting the amendment process in the Committee of the Whole House on the State of the

11. A rule can be amended on the floor if the House first votes not to order the previous question on it, which does not happen very often for reasons we shall discuss. The majority floor manager also can offer an amendment or, in theory, yield to another member to do so.

12. Under Reed and his immediate successors, when the committee first gained the power it continues to exercise, the Speaker served as its chairman. Speakers exercised much of their power through the committee, and they did so directly and overtly. But the Speaker was deprived of his chairmanship as part of the revolt of 1910–11 against "Uncle Joe" Cannon.

13. Before 1965, it sometimes was necessary to obtain a special rule from the Rules Committee in order to go to conference with the Senate on a measure both houses already had passed, although in different forms. The House now can agree to a motion for this purpose without recourse to the Rules Committee if the motion is authorized by the committee of jurisdiction. See Rule XX, clause 1 (*House Rules and Manual*, pp. 567–69).

Union (commonly called Committee of the Whole), where the House conducts much of its important legislative business.

This Committee of the Whole, to which all members of the House belong and which meets on the House floor, is really the House meeting temporarily in the form of a committee. The House "resolves," or transforms, itself into Committee of the Whole to consider an individual bill or resolution, and the Speaker appoints another member of the majority to serve as the committee's chairman during its deliberations on that measure. The reason for this parliamentary metamorphosis lies in the difference between the legislative procedures that apply "in the House" and those that typically govern consideration in Committee of the Whole. Almost every major bill and resolution that reaches the House floor is considered in Committee of the Whole because its procedures are better suited to widespread participation by House members.[14]

The most important advantages of the Committee of the Whole flow from its more equitable and flexible procedures governing debate and amendment. "In the House" each member may speak for an hour on every bill, on every amendment, and on every other debatable question that arises, until a majority votes to order the previous question. The effect of this vote usually is to bring the House to an immediate vote on whatever it has been considering, with no further debate and with no opportunity for anyone to amend it. And in practice, the House almost always agrees to this motion after no more than one hour of debate, without having entertained any floor amendments except those proposed by the committee of jurisdiction.

In Committee of the Whole, on the other hand, there are two distinct stages of consideration. First, there is a period of an hour or more for general debate, during which members discuss the circumstances provoking legislative action, the state of current law, and the provisions of the bill, its strengths and weaknesses, and the wisdom of enacting it. Thereafter, each amendment to the bill that members propose is debated under the "five-minute rule."[15] Clause 5(a) of Rule XXIII permits one five-

14. Since 1794 House rules have required that certain measures be considered in Committee of the Whole. Rule XXIII, clause 3, now states in part that "all motions or propositions involving a tax or charge upon the people, all proceedings touching appropriations of money, or bills making appropriations of money, or property, or requiring such appropriation to be made . . . shall be first considered in a Committee of the Whole. . . ." (*House Rules and Manual*, pp. 613–15).

15. There is no requirement that the committee begin and complete its work on a bill in one sitting. Instead, the committee can vote to "rise" at any time, transforming itself back into the House, and then resolve back into Committee of the Whole on a later day to resume

minute speech in favor of an amendment and one against it. Other members then can speak for five minutes each by offering "pro forma amendments"—motions to "strike the last word" or the "requisite number of words"—and no member can speak for longer without the unanimous consent of all the other members who are on the floor.[16]

In Committee of the Whole, members usually have to offer their amendments to each section (or title) of a bill in turn. And as the committee considers each first-degree amendment (which proposes to change the text of the measure itself), members can propose second-degree amendments to perfect it, substitutes for it, and amendments to the substitutes. Each substitute or second-degree amendment also is debatable under the five-minute rule. Finally, after members have voted on the last amendment to the last part of the bill, the committee does not vote on the measure itself. Instead, the committee "rises" and reports the bill back to the House with the amendments to which it has agreed. But the Committee of the Whole, like the House's standing committees, cannot actually amend a measure; only the House, sitting as the House, has that authority. The amendments adopted in Committee of the Whole are only recommendations to the House, which must vote on them again. The House typically agrees to all the amendments by a single voice vote before voting on final passage of the bill as it now has been amended.[17] Any amendments that were offered but rejected in Committee of the Whole are not reported back to the House, so they are not subject to a second vote.[18]

By controlling the amendments that members may offer during the

---

consideration of the same bill. For example, the House may resolve into Committee of the Whole on a Monday, when some members are still in their districts, but only for purposes of general debate that is unlikely to involve any record votes. After general debate, the committee rises, postponing debate and votes on amendments until later in the week.

16. The Committee of the Whole can control its deliberations by agreeing to a unanimous consent request or a nondebatable motion to close the debate on a pending amendment (and any amendments to it) or on whatever part of the measure is then open to amendment (and any amendments to it). Such a request or motion can propose to end the debate immediately, at a certain time, or after a specified additional period of time for debate.

17. On the amending process, see Stanley Bach, "The Amending Process in the House of Representatives," report 87-778 GOV (Congressional Research Service, September 22, 1987); and Oleszek, *Congressional Procedures and the Policy Process*, pp. 132–49.

18. An amendment rejected in Committee of the Whole sometimes is presented to the House for another vote, immediately before the vote on final passage, as part of a recommittal motion. This motion typically proposes to recommit the bill to the committee that considered it originally, with instructions that the committee report it back to the House "forthwith" with a specified amendment. If the House agrees to this motion, it resumes consideration of the bill immediately and then votes on the amendment before voting on the bill itself.

amendment process in Committee of the Whole, special rules can pro-
foundly affect the policy decisions the House has the opportunity to
make. So designing these resolutions truly is a strategic process. Committee and party leaders, as well as other House members, make requests
of the Rules Committee and attempt to influence its decisions in anticipation of the amendments that would or would not be in order on the
floor without the committee's intervention. By the same token, the members of Rules anticipate the reactions of other representatives as they
make their own strategic calculations. The committee always must bear
in mind that the resolutions it reports require approval by a majority of
the House, and, like other congressional committees, it is anxious to
avoid floor defeats. But unlike most other committee members, the Democrats and Republicans on Rules also have a special responsibility to promote, or at least accommodate, the interests of their parties as well as the
work of the House. For these reasons, changes in special rules, which are
the products of this interactive process, reflect the changing dynamics of
congressional decisionmaking.

Our "Order of Business"

This study focuses primarily on the Rules Committee from 1975 to 1986,
during the 94th through the 99th Congresses. In chapter 2, we discuss
some of the reasons why Rules now makes its decisions in a more complex institutional setting and a more uncertain political and strategic environment and why the committee has sought to adapt to new opportunities, constraints, and demands. Then chapter 3 characterizes the special
rules the committee has granted during this period. We demonstrate the
inadequacy of the conventional distinctions among open, modified, and
closed rules; identify the procedural innovations that the committee has
developed; and discuss some of the ways in which these innovations have
helped committees and subcommittees, majority party leaders, and all
members to cope with the increased uncertainties and challenges of
decisionmaking in the House. In chapter 4, we examine some of the
ways in which members' expectations, attitudes, and behavior also have
changed, as they vote on special rules and propose amendments to the
bills and resolutions these rules bring to the House floor. And finally, in
chapter 5, we consider the implications of all these developments for the
House's majority party leadership, the committee system, and the Rules
Committee itself.

CHAPTER TWO

Change and Uncertainty
in the 1970s

THE RULES COMMITTEE stands at the crossroads of the legislative process in the House. Nearly all major legislation passes through Suite H313, its hearing room in the Capitol, so most members make their way there at one time or another to ask the committee to grant them favored treatment or somehow to protect their interests in its special rules. As a result, significant changes in the House's membership, organization, or procedures are almost certain to touch the Rules Committee sooner or later.

Four such developments touched the committee directly during the 1970s, complicating its work and affecting the strategic decisions that were embodied in the special rules it reported. First, a pair of changes in voting procedures altered both the tactics and the outcomes of the amending process in Committee of the Whole. Second, authorizing multiple referrals of legislation to two or more standing committees increased the likelihood of conflict between (or among) them and created the need for new techniques to manage intercommittee conflict. Third, the devolution of legislative influence and activity from House committees and their chairmen to their subcommittees undermined the reasons and incentives for deference to committee positions when their bills reached the floor. And fourth, and partly as a consequence of the first three developments, the House experienced a striking increase in the number of floor amendments offered and adopted as challenges to committee proposals.

These internal developments were partly provoked, and certainly reinforced, by changes in Congress's political environment. In rapid succession, new and divisive issues—such as the Vietnam War, consumer protection, environmental quality, energy dependence, Watergate, and CIA abuses of power—became inescapable and increasingly prominent elements of the congressional agenda. And as the role of the federal government continued to expand during the post–Great Society years, so too did the number, resources, and variety of groups that sought to influence congressional decisions. Many of the new issues to which the House had to react cut across traditional lines of partisan cleavage and committee jurisdiction, sometimes creating deep intraparty divisions and leading many members to question the conventional ways of doing things in the House. Indeed, in 1974, the aftershocks of Watergate swept into the House a new class of freshmen Democrats, who brought to Washington a perceived mandate for change and provided the needed votes for the major series of reform decisions made by the Democratic Caucus just before the 94th Congress convened.

A principal result of all this was greater uncertainty in the House. Individually and collectively, these internal and external developments made floor activity and decisions less predictable by increasing the number of effective participants, expanding the range and altering the balance of interests that members advocated through the amending process, and enlarging the variety of issues raised and alternatives presented on the floor of the House. The range of possible policy outcomes increased while the ability of participants to anticipate outcomes decreased. In other words, it became harder to know which members would propose what amendments and how likely they were to win. The same developments also posed particular challenges for the Rules Committee, which itself was the subject of several significant reforms during the 1970s. The committee responded by devising innovative ways to assert its own authority while serving the interests of the majority party and the needs of the House.

Recorded Voting and the Amendment Process

Among the most important procedural changes that eventually were reflected in the changing practices of the Rules Committee were two alterations made during the early 1970s in the rules governing voting on the House floor. In 1971 the House implemented a provision of the Legislative Reorganization Act of 1970 permitting recorded teller votes on amendments in Committee of the Whole. Two years later, the House began to use its new electronic voting system to conduct these votes, as well as the roll call ("yea and nay") votes taken in the House itself. Together, these procedural changes provoked a notable change in members' behavior on the floor.

As the brief summary in chapter 1 indicates, the amendment process in Committee of the Whole is a particularly important stage of the House's legislative proceedings. It is during this stage that the House effectively decides on amendments to the major legislation it considers. Amendments adopted in Committee of the Whole rarely are rejected thereafter by the House, and amendments defeated in Committee of the Whole rarely are revived successfully when the committee reports its recommendations to the House. Yet before 1971 members' votes on amendments in Committee of the Whole were not recorded individually and published in the *Congressional Record*. The Constitution (article I, section 5) gives one-fifth of the members present the right to order "the yeas and nays," meaning a roll call vote, on any question, but this right does not extend to votes occurring in committees of the House, including the Committee of the Whole. Before implementation of the 1970 act, the Committee of the Whole acted on amendments by voice or division (standing) votes or by "teller votes," in which the members favoring an amendment walk up the center aisle of the chamber, followed by those opposed to it, and are counted by two members appointed to count or "tell" them.[1]

Teller votes produced accurate counts of the total number of members voting for and against amendments but no official record of their individual positions. Anyone wanting to know how members voted on a particular amendment had to observe the vote as it took place. In their biography of Sam Rayburn, for example, D. B. Hardeman and Donald Bacon describe the scene in 1935 as the Committee of the Whole voted on a critical amendment to a bill that Rayburn, then chairman of the Committee on Interstate and Foreign Commerce, was managing on the floor:

> When the House met on the day of decision, twenty-six Scripps-Howard reporters filed into the House press gallery. To assure getting good seats, they arrived four hours early. Each was responsible for identifying certain representatives as they marched between the tellers. Reporter Charter Heslep, who knew all of the members, knelt on a front-row stool and called the name and state of each. The next day, in a classic example of journalistic enterprise, Scripps-Howard newspapers across the country printed the unofficial tally. Members were furious.[2]

Presumably, "members were furious" because they had been denied the protection of anonymity that they were used to enjoying. After all, the

---

1. House rules still permit such unrecorded or "walking" teller votes, but they have become quite rare.

2. D. B. Hardeman and Donald C. Bacon, *Rayburn: A Biography* (Austin: Texas Monthly Press, 1987), p. 185.

Constitution did not prohibit public tallies of teller votes; it only failed to require them. And it was not by chance or oversight that the House had never adopted a rule authorizing them.

Most members evidently found it advantageous to protect their votes on amendments from public scrutiny, until July 27, 1970, when Representative Thomas P. (Tip) O'Neill, Jr., then a midranking member of the Rules Committee, successfully offered a floor amendment to the Legislative Reorganization Act. His amendment permitted twenty members (one-fifth of a quorum in Committee of the Whole) to require a recorded teller vote on any amendment. In support of his proposal, O'Neill argued:

> If the work of legislation can be done shrouded in secrecy and hidden from the public, then we are eroding the confidence of the public in ourselves and in our institutions.
>
> Often the most important parts of a bill—and usually the most controversial sections—are decided upon in amendment form. And there is no record of how Members vote.
>
> The ABM, the SST, the invasion of Cambodia, were all dealt with in the Committee of the Whole, in nonrecorded teller votes. . . .
>
> The secrecy of the Committee of the Whole has allowed too many Members to duck issues, to avoid the perils of controversial votes. But that is not in the spirit of this Nation, nor of this Congress.[3]

Before recorded voting was adopted for the Committee of the Whole, members were far more accountable to their colleagues than to their constituents for their votes on amendments. This situation undoubtedly worked to the advantage of committee chairmen, who naturally opposed most amendments to the bills their committees had reported, who could observe how their colleagues voted, and whose power had not yet been diluted by the reforms that were to follow during the 1970s. Thus opponents of the committee's position were at a distinct disadvantage. Members could conclude that it was pointless or even self-defeating to offer their own amendments and dangerous to support other members' floor amendments, and so stand against a committee chairman whose assistance and support they were sure to need at some time in the future. Beginning in 1971, however, when the O'Neill amendment became effective, representatives had to reconsider how they calculated the effects

3. *Congressional Record* (July 27, 1970), p. 25796.

of proposing and voting on amendments. There now could be a public record for constituents to study and for challengers to criticize. The availability of recorded teller votes gave members new incentives to offer amendments in Committee of the Whole—to stake out public positions, for example. And making members publicly accountable for their votes on amendments surely made them more inclined to support amendments they believed their constituents would support, even though it meant opposing powerful committee leaders.

The 1970 change in voting rules also affected members' expectations and calculations in another, related way. Before this rule change took effect, members did not have much incentive to be on the floor during the amending process when bills from committees on which they did not sit were being considered. They usually could expect that the committee's position would prevail without major change. And they also knew that their votes would not be recorded on whatever amendments were offered, so neither their positions nor their presence or absence would be a matter of public record. Thus committee members, who were more likely to be present because of their interest and investment in their bills, often had a disproportionate influence on the outcomes of division or teller votes on amendments, because there was little if any time for other members to come to the floor to vote. And members' appreciation of this situation made it that much less likely that they would propose floor amendments and win. Recorded teller voting, on the other hand, gave all members time and incentives to come to the floor from their offices or committee rooms during a vote. The fate of floor amendments now would be decided by the overwhelming majority of members, not by a self-selected minority who chose to be on or near the floor when votes began. A change in voting procedures could affect participation, which in turn could affect outcomes.

During consideration of O'Neill's amendment, therefore, members debated not only *whether* votes on amendments should be recorded in Committee of the Whole, but also *how* recorded teller votes and roll call votes should be conducted. Immediately after agreeing to the amendment, the members considered and approved another proposal, presented by Robert McClory, Republican from Illinois, authorizing the installation of an electronic voting system to be used for conducting recorded teller votes on amendments in Committee of the Whole as well as roll call votes and quorum calls in the House. As a result, almost all votes of public record that have been ordered since 1973, when the new system became operational, have been taken "by electronic device," and the time needed for each vote has been roughly one-half of that formerly consumed by a traditional call of the roll.[4]

One incentive for authorizing the electronic voting system was the concern that permitting recorded teller votes might slow down the House's legislative business. O'Neill suggested that this would not be a problem, that most amendments would not provoke recorded votes:

> During the year 1968 there were 63 teller votes. If one had been able to ask for teller votes with clerks during the year 1968, I say they would have only been asked for about 15 times. There were 15 really national, earth-shaking decisions on which the people at home should have known how you felt about them and how I voted and how you voted.[5]

But the future Speaker's expectation that there would not be many demands for recorded teller votes was not borne out. During the 92d Congress (1971–72), there were nearly 200 such votes, almost all of which were votes on amendments in Committee of the Whole.[6] The number of these votes exceeded 400 in five of the next seven Congresses, as table 2-1 indicates, reaching a maximum of 505 during 1977–78. The ability to put oneself, and especially one's opponents, on public record, coupled with the convenience of electronic voting, evidently was an almost irresistible temptation.[7] And as we shall document later in this chapter, these

4. Members generally have a minimum of fifteen minutes to reach the floor and cast their votes by electronic device, but there is no maximum time allowed for voting. This became the cause of considerable controversy in October 1987, when the Speaker left a vote open for much longer than fifteen minutes and the House passed a reconciliation bill by a one-vote margin. *Congressional Record*, daily edition (October 29, 1987), pp. H9446–47.

5. Ibid. (July 27, 1970), p. 25797. The reference to "teller votes with clerks" is to the procedure for conducting recorded teller votes during the two years before installation of the electronic voting system.

6. Members may demand recorded teller votes in the House but they rarely do so. It usually is much easer for them to achieve the same purpose—requiring members' positions to be publicly recorded—by insisting on a roll call vote. Whenever a member objects to a voice or division vote in the House on the ground that a quorum is not present, which usually is the case, and makes a point of order to that effect, House rules require that a roll call vote occur automatically.

7. The percentage of floor amendments decided by voice vote stayed within the range of 55 to 65 percent during the 91st-94th Congresses (1969–76), suggesting (though not demonstrating) that members were demanding recorded teller votes on the kinds of amendments that had been decided before by division or walking teller votes. See Steven S. Smith, "Revolution in the House: Why Don't We Do It on the Floor?" Brookings Discussion Paper in Governmental Studies no. 5 (Brookings, September 1986), table 2.

TABLE 2-1. Recorded Teller and Roll Call Votes in the House of Representatives, 92d–99th Congresses (1971–86)

Congress	Recorded teller votes	Roll call votes
92d (1971–72)	193	456
93d (1973–74)	446	632
94th (1975–76)	463	810
95th (1977–78)	505	1,035
96th (1979–80)	497	779
97th (1981–82)	293	519
98th (1983–84)	382	524
99th (1985–86)	441	479

SOURCE: Roger H. Davidson and Carol Hardy, "Indicators of House of Representatives Workload and Activity," report 87-492S (Congressional Research Service, June 8, 1987), p. 65.

two changes in voting procedures were accompanied by, and probably were necessary conditions for, a dramatic increase in the total number of floor amendments proposed, whether they were accepted or rejected by voice, division, or teller vote.

Committee and floor leaders had to expect, therefore, that the bills they brought to the floor were likely to confront more amendments, that the amending process often would consume more time, and that the outcomes of votes in Committee of the Whole would be less predictable. Anticipating dangers, planning tactics, and predicting outcomes all became far more difficult as the number of potential participants increased. Faced with greater possibilities of miscalculation, both committee leaders and party leaders had good reasons to seek help from the Rules Committee to protect them from the dangers they could anticipate and to minimize the dangers they could not. Yet at much the same time, there were pressures on the committee from quite a different direction—rank-and-file Democrats who were asserting that it should be more responsive to Democratic Caucus preferences. To caucus members, the Rules Committee offered a way they could protect themselves against committee majorities and even their own committee chairmen when they could not rely on their party leaders. It was to this complex mixture of interests and demands that the committee had to respond.

Multiple Referrals and Intercommittee Conflict

Three years after authorizing recorded votes in Committee of the Whole, the House adopted H. Res. 988, the Committee Reform Amendments of 1974, based on recommendations by the Select Committee on Committees (known informally as the Bolling Committee, after its chairman, Richard Bolling) and a Democratic Caucus committee chaired by Julia Butler Hansen.[8] Among the issues this resolution addressed were a related pair of perennial problems: assuring that standing committee jurisdictions were well adapted to the issues of the day and seeing that they created an equitable distribution of work and influence among the House's committees. Many issues of the late 1960s and early 1970s—such as environmental protection, energy, consumer protection, and transportation—cut across several committees' existing jurisdictions. The result was intercommittee competition or conflict and sometimes incoherent policy or even no policy at all.

The select committee recommended various jurisdictional changes, but recognized that reshuffling subjects among committees was not a full or lasting solution to either problem. The committee's report stated:

> The select committee has no illusions . . . that it has been able (or in fact, that it is humanly possible) to eliminate overlapping committee responsibilities. Considering the interdependencies of governmental activities, these overlaps will continue to be a fact of life in the House. Not only are they unavoidable, but in some cases they are desirable as well—to promote flexible consideration of issues, and to permit Members with varying specialties to make their distinctive contributions.[9]

Instead of attempting vainly to eliminate jurisdictional overlaps, the resolution proposed that the House not merely recognize their inevitability but actually take advantage of them by permitting multiple referrals of legislation. The House agreed, and amended Rule XI to permit the Speaker to refer the same measure to two or more committees concurrently or sequentially or to split it into the parts falling within each committee's jurisdiction. Bills and resolutions that were subject to multiple referral increased from 6 percent of all measures introduced in the 94th Congress (1975–76), when the Speaker's new referral authority became

8. On the work of the select committee, see Roger H. Davidson and Walter J. Oleszek, *Congress Against Itself* (Indiana University Press, 1977).

9. *Committee Reform Amendments of 1974*, H. Rept. 93-916, 93 Cong. 2 sess. (Government Printing Office, 1974), pt. 2, p. 55. Many of the select committee's jurisdictional proposals failed to survive review by the caucus committee and the House, as did a proposal that the Rules Committee become a forum for resolving jurisdictional conflicts.

effective, to more than 10 percent in the 95th (1977–78) and nearly 12 percent in the 96th Congress (1979–80).[10]

In permitting multiple referrals, the House presumably hoped to reduce, if not eliminate, disputes among committees with legitimate claims to jurisdiction over the same measure, even if the price of harmony was the addition of a new source of delay to an already tortuous process. In many cases, however, authorizing two or more committees to recommend amendments to the same legislative proposal has created new opportunities for intercommittee conflict over jurisdiction and policy.

The possibility of multiple referrals has encouraged some committees to assert jurisdictional claims they had neglected previously and other committees to stake claims that are defensible but marginal. In either event, it is the Speaker who must decide among the contending claims, and he cannot always do so to everyone's satisfaction. In many instances too, multiple referrals have created the virtual certainty of intercommittee disagreements over legislation. These disagreements can cause personal and institutional friction among senior committee leaders and especially their chairmen, highlight or even exacerbate divisions within the Democratic majority, lead to public contests on the House floor between incompatible committee positions, and in the process create opportunities for the Republican minority to exercise greater influence over the House's decisions. In such cases, multiple referrals can create both political and procedural problems for the Rules Committee.

Not all multiply referred bills pose such potential problems, of course. Most of them never emerge from committee and, of those that do, some are of genuine interest to only one committee; the second committee does not oppose the bill, but may assert jurisdiction only to protect its claim to subsequent bills on the same subject. Sometimes one of the committees agrees to amendments that reflect the concerns or incorporate the recommendations of the other or that narrow the scope of the bill so that it no longer overlaps jurisdictional lines. In any of these cases, the multiple referral does not create any particular problem for the Rules Committee. All the committee need do is write a special rule that divides control of the time for general debate among the committees.

Our primary interest here is not in the sheer number of multiply referred bills, but in the effect of multiple referrals on intercommittee relations, the Rules Committee, and members' decisions on the floor. For this reason, we shall look more closely at what we designate multiple-

10. Roger H. Davidson, Walter J. Oleszek, and Thomas Kephart, "One Bill, Many Committees: Multiple Referrals in the U.S. House of Representatives," *Legislative Studies Quarterly*, vol. 13 (February 1988), p. 7.

TABLE 2-2. Single- and Multiple-Committee Measures Subject to
Special Rules, 94th–99th Congresses (1975–86)
Percent

	Congress					
Type of measure	94th ('75–'76)	95th ('77–'78)	96th ('79–'80)	97th ('81–'82)	98th ('83–'84)	99th ('85–'86)
Single-committee	89.9	82.8	86.2	76.9	80.8	79.2
Multiple-committee	6.9	16.1	12.7	19.2	17.6	19.8
Other^a	3.2	1.1	1.1	3.8	1.6	1.0
N	248	186	181	104	125	101

SOURCES: Final *Calendars* of the House of Representatives and the Committee on Rules.
a. Includes, for example, measures considered under special rules in the House under the hour rule, rather than in Committee of the Whole, and measures considered without having been referred to committee.

committee measures—bills and resolutions that reached the floor and in which two or more committees demonstrated an active jurisdictional or policy concern, either by reporting the measure or by receiving control of time for general debate.[11] The number of such multiple-committee bills that received special rules for floor consideration is relatively small, growing from twelve in the 94th Congress to twenty-two in the 95th and remaining within that range for the following eight years. As table 2-2 indicates, on the other hand, multiple-committee measures did constitute roughly one-fifth of the Rules Committee's work load between 1981 and 1986.[12] Moreover, precisely because of the scope of these bills, they are disproportionately likely to be important and controversial and, therefore, a problem for the Rules Committee.

When two or more committees do mark up the same bill or find themselves at odds over it for whatever reasons, it is the Rules Committee that often has to cope with the consequences. For example, the committees of jurisdiction may not even agree on whether or when the bill should come to the floor, much less on how it should be considered. The committee generally has been unwilling to report a special rule sending a bill

11. By this definition, not all multiply referred measures are multiple-committee measures. On the other hand, virtually all multiple-committee measures are multiply referred.

12. Although we are not concerned here with the Rules Committee's original jurisdiction over measures proposing changes in House rules, multiple referrals also affected this secondary aspect of the committee's work because of the increasing number of bills that included expedited procedures to govern consideration of specific kinds of measures, especially resolutions of approval or disapproval. The committee eventually began to assert its claim to original jurisdiction over bills containing these provisions because of a concern among some committee members that the proliferation of such rulemaking provisions was undermining the committee's authority and the Democratic leadership's control over the floor agenda.

to the floor until all the committees of jurisdiction have reported it or agreed to be discharged from considering it further (even though Rules has the power to extract a measure from the control of another standing committee).[13] And then, when committees report conflicting recommendations on the same bill, which must be resolved on the floor if not before, they may disagree as well about the terms and conditions of the special rule for debating and amending it. As an arm of the majority party leadership, the Rules Democrats have an interest in preventing such intercommittee conflict from dividing and embarrassing their party and damaging the bill's prospects for passage.[14] And in their capacity as Rules Committee members, they also need to accommodate conflicting committee interests as best they can in order to protect against one or more of the committees opposing their special rule on the floor.

Intercommittee conflict flowing from multiple referrals can result in more complicated special rules, which, some members complain, work to the advantage of one committee over another. In drafting the rule for a multiply referred bill, the Rules Committee is more likely than in other cases to have plausible alternative arrangements from which to choose as it selects the text to be amended on the floor, allocates control of the time for general debate, arranges for votes on the committees' recommendations, and disposes of germaneness and other procedural problems that multiple referrals can provoke.

If the committees propose mutually acceptable and compatible amendments, usually on different subjects, Rules confronts only a technical procedural problem that it usually can resolve without controversy. When an intercommittee conflict cannot be settled in any other way, however, Rules must structure an amending process that allows members to choose among the alternatives. And in doing so, it is often difficult, if not impossible, to avoid giving (or appearing to give) a tactical advantage to one side or the other. The special rule may state, for example, that one committee's proposal shall be considered as an amendment to the other's; if so, members must reject the first proposal if they are to have a chance to vote on the second, unless the Rules Committee proposes even more complicated and unusual procedures. So multiply referred bills are more

13. Roger H. Davidson and Walter J. Oleszek, "From Monopoly to Interaction: Changing Patterns in Committee Management of Legislation in the House," paper prepared for the 1987 annual meeting of the Midwest Political Science Association, pp. 29–30.

14. While the committee is not wholly subordinate to the leadership, Republican observers challenge characterizing their relationship as an alliance. As one of them has commented anonymously, "We're not talking U.S. and Great Britain here; it's more like the USSR and Latvia."

likely than others to enmesh Rules in controversies involving committees and subcommittees, and especially their chairmen, which the committee cannot always prevent from spilling over onto the House floor.

Whatever the virtues and advantages of multiple referrals, then, they certainly have complicated the task of the Rules Committee in designing many of the most important special rules it has reported since 1975.

Committee Decentralization and Bill Management

To complicate matters further, House Democratic leaders, as well as Rules Committee members of both parties, have had to confront some of the consequences of a series of changes the Democratic Caucus made in its rules during the 1970s. These changes significantly redistributed resources and influence between House committees and their subcommittees. Shortly after the House authorized recorded teller votes, thereby reducing members' inclination to defer to committee positions, the caucus set in train a series of developments that further undercut both the rationale and the incentives for such deference.[15] These developments have become familiar to observers of the House under such rubrics as "subcommittee government,"[16] as have the subsequent concerns that decentralization and democratization have bred a degree of fragmentation that makes coherent policymaking even more difficult in what was already a disjointed institution. One result has been a significant movement in the locus of legislative activity—hearings and markups—from the committee to the subcommittee level.[17] Evidence is now beginning to emerge that this shift in activity also reflects a shift in the locus of decisionmaking, with more legislative policy choices being made by subcommittees without being reversed by their parent committees.[18]

15. These developments are discussed in Norman J. Ornstein, "Causes and Consequences of Congressional Change: Subcommittee Reforms in the House of Representatives, 1970–73" in Ornstein, ed., *Congress in Change: Evolution and Reform* (Praeger, 1975), pp. 88–114; and David W. Rohde, "Committee Reform in the House of Representatives and the Subcommittee Bill of Rights," *Annals of the American Academy of Political and Social Science*, vol. 411 (January 1974), pp. 39–47.

16. See, for example, Roger H. Davidson, "Subcommittee Government: New Channels for Policy Making," in Thomas E. Mann and Norman J. Ornstein, eds., *The New Congress* (Washington, D.C.: American Enterprise Institute for Public Policy Research, 1981), pp. 99–133.

17. Steven S. Smith and Christopher J. Deering, *Committees in Congress* (Washington, D.C.: CQ Press, 1984), pp. 125–65.

18. See, for example, Richard L. Hall and C. Lawrence Evans, "The Role of the Subcommittee in Committee Decision Making: An Exploration," paper prepared for the 1985 annual meeting of the American Political Science Association.

It should not be surprising, therefore, that subcommittee chairmen have begun to play a more active role on the floor during consideration of the measures they reported. Bill managers have been coming from the ranks of subcommittee chairmen in increasing numbers. In the 89th Congress (1965–66), for example, less than half (42 percent) of the measures reaching the floor were managed by subcommittee chairmen, with most of the remainder managed by full committee chairmen.[19] By the 95th Congress (1977–78), subcommittee chairmen managed fully two-thirds of all bills on the floor. This trend actually reflects a stated policy of the Democratic Caucus; its Rule 39 states that "the chairmen of full committees shall, insofar as practicable, permit subcommittee chairmen to handle on the floor legislation from their respective subcommittees."[20]

This development on the House floor, which may have been an inevitable result of the redistribution of influence within House committees, has only added to the problems faced by the Speaker and other House Democrats who share his leadership perspective. In addition to their policy goals, majority party leaders have an institutional interest in moving legislation on and off the House floor with reasonable efficiency and a related political interest in seeing committees' positions, usually reflecting their Democratic majorities, prevail on the floor. The prevalence of subcommittee chairmen among bill managers has made both of these interests more difficult to promote.

Subcommittees tend to have less experienced leadership and membership than full committees; high rates of subcommittee turnover have become a striking characteristic of the contemporary House.[21] This development has served to undermine two of the primary reasons why members traditionally had been inclined to defer to committee recommendations on the floor. First, bill managers less often have established reputations for long experience in their positions and acknowledged expertise in the subjects within their jurisdictions; members in their first or second term as subcommittee chairmen normally cannot make a claim to wisdom that their colleagues find compelling. Second, the high levels of turnover among subcommittee chairmen give less cause for members to defer to subcommittee recommendations in anticipation that they will

19. Smith and Deering, p. 195.
20. "Preamble and Rules of the Democratic Caucus," rev., 100th Congress, February 19, 1987, p. 14.
21. Stanley Bach, "Membership, Committees, and Change in the House of Representatives," paper prepared for the 1984 annual meeting of the American Political Science Association.

want the assistance or cooperation of the same subcommittee leaders in the future.[22]

In addition, subcommittees almost inevitably are less likely than full committees to accurately reflect the distribution of preferences in the House at large. The small size of most subcommittees increases the likelihood that they will be unrepresentative of all 435 members. Furthermore, Democratic committee members have the right, under Democratic Caucus rules, to select at least some subcommittee assignments, and Republican members' preferences normally are accommodated through a somewhat less formal process. So while subcommittees may be "little legislatures," they are not the House writ small. Nor do full committees, with their larger memberships and presumably broader perspectives, always review and revise subcommittee bills with care. There is a natural tendency for members of one subcommittee to defer to the members of others as a way of protecting and enhancing the influence of each subcommittee within its limited domain.

At the same time that more of the responsibilities for bill management on the floor were being assumed by subcommittees and their chairmen, other developments during the 1970s were giving Republicans and rank-and-file members more impressive resources with which to devise and promote their own amendments and generally to participate more effectively on the floor. Minority party contingents on committees were guaranteed their own staffs, and the personal staffs of all members grew. Whereas most members once could afford to hire only one legislative assistant, the personal staffs of many representatives expanded to include a legislative director, several legislative assistants, and legislative correspondents. In addition, members also benefited from an increase in the number, capacity, and services of the congressional support agencies (Congressional Budget Office, Congressional Research Service, General Accounting Office, and Office of Technology Assessment). In short, members with no relevant committee assignment and little floor experience gained the capacity to prepare amendments and speeches on topics that

22. Shepsle and Weingast, on the other hand, emphasize the ability of subcommittees to protect existing programs and benefits. "The influence of these subcommittees is both subtle and typically overlooked because their strongest power—the capacity to block proposed changes in programs within their jurisdiction—need not be actively or publicly exercised in order to be effective. In other words, subcommittees are powerful because they can say no and do nothing." Kenneth A. Shepsle and Barry R. Weingast, "Policy Consequences of Government by Congressional Subcommittees," in C. Lowell Harriss, ed., *Control of Federal Spending*, Proceedings of the Academy of Political Science, vol. 35, no. 4 (1985), p. 115.

previously had been beyond their reach. Consequently, floor managers had much more difficulty identifying all the directions from which trouble might emerge on the House floor.

Moreover, because subcommittees have more limited jurisdictions than full committees, subcommittee leaders have fewer occasions to come before the Rules Committee and then manage bills on the floor. Under these circumstances, it is not surprising that Rules Committee hearings increasingly began to take on the flavor of dress rehearsals. As Bruce Oppenheimer has pointed out, bill managers found Rules Committee hearings to be a place to practice the arguments they would be making on the floor and to receive a preview from Rules members of the arguments they would hear from others.[23] Indeed, as dress rehearsals, Rules Committee hearings became a more vital source of information for bill managers, Rules Committee members, and party leaders. Nonetheless, amendment sponsors were not obligated to inform Rules or the bill managers of their intentions unless they expected the committee to propose that floor amendments be restricted. So dress rehearsals by themselves helped chairmen and ranking members perfect their arguments, but did not eliminate uncertainty about who would offer what amendments and with what results.

In the ordinary course of events, the Rules Committee, and especially its Democratic majority, prefers to rely on the members requesting a rule to recommend what provisions it should include and to alert the committee (and through it, the Democratic leadership) to any possible political or procedural pitfalls that might lie in wait on the floor. Committee decentralization and the changing pattern of bill management has made this a much riskier practice. As one senior Rules Committee staff member pointed out in a recent interview, inexperienced subcommittee chairmen are "less able to anticipate problems" on the floor. As a result, the Rules Committee has received less guidance from prospective bill managers who are seeking special rules and has had to become more cautious in evaluating the recommendations and political intelligence they do offer.

Instead, inexperienced subcommittee chairmen have had reason to request rules that would help them as bill managers by minimizing their uncertainties about the procedural and policy problems they might confront on the floor. The Congressional Budget Act of 1974, for example, and the complex procedures that grew up around it, made it increasingly difficult for even the most diligent chairmen to be certain that their bills

---

23. Bruce I. Oppenheimer, "The Rules Committee: New Arm of Leadership in a Decentralized House," in Lawrence C. Dodd and Bruce I. Oppenheimer, eds., *Congress Reconsidered* (Praeger, 1977), pp. 96–116.

were immune from any points of order on the floor. The still more complex restrictions of the Gramm-Rudman-Hollings acts of 1985 and 1987 only added to the uncertainty. The Rules Committee could help by granting waivers to protect bills against points of order. As we shall show in chapter 3, the committee could protect Democratic bill managers against the unknown by drafting special rules under which there could be no unexpected amendments to take them by surprise on the floor.

Floor Amendments: Expansion and Reaction

As noted earlier, members were not slow to capitalize on the opportunity given them by the 1970 O'Neill amendment to demand recorded votes in Committee of the Whole. But the growth in recorded teller votes was only one manifestation of a dramatic surge in amending activity on the floor that had begun earlier, but escalated with the advent of electronic voting in 1973.[24]

Table 2-3 presents data on the total number of House floor amendments, not just those decided by recorded teller and roll call votes. Note that representatives proposed slightly more than 400 amendments during the 84th Congress (1955–56), roughly twice as many during the 90th–92d Congresses, and more than three times that number during each of the Congresses since 1973 for which data are available. Particularly noteworthy is the difference between the 92d Congress (1971–72), when slightly fewer than 800 amendments were presented, and the following Congress in 1973–74, when that total increased by roughly 80 percent to more than 1,400 amendments. Although the lack of comparable data for the 97th and 98th Congresses makes our inferences and conclusions tentative, the level of amending activity on the House floor appears to have peaked during the 95th Congress (1977–78). Perhaps House committees became more attuned to the prospect of floor amendments, eliminating the need for them by taking better account of members' interests and preferences during committee markup. But, as we shall discuss later, there are reasons to think that the decline in amending activity during

24. See Stanley Bach, "Representatives and Committees on the Floor: Amendments to Appropriations Bills in the House of Representatives, 1963–1982," *Congress and the Presidency*, vol. 13 (Spring 1986), pp. 41–58; Steven S. Smith, "Decision Making on the House Floor," paper prepared for the 1986 annual meeting of the American Political Science Association; Smith, "Going to the Floor: Changing Patterns of Participation in the U.S. House of Representatives, 1955–1986," Brookings Discussion Paper in Governmental Studies no. 13 (Brookings, September 1987); and Smith, *Call to Order: Floor Politics in the House and Senate* (Brookings, forthcoming).

TABLE 2-3. Floor Amendments in the House, Selected Congresses
(1955–86)

Congress	Total number of amendments offered	Number of amendments offered to "key vote" measures[a]
84th (1955–56)	405	99
86th (1959–60)	446	147
88th (1963–64)	614	258
90th (1967–68)	847	165
91st (1969–70)	877	177
92d (1971–72)	792	179
93d (1973–74)	1,425	366
94th (1975–76)	1,366	360
95th (1977–78)	1,695	428
96th (1979–80)	1,377	355
97th (1981–82)	n.a.	349
98th (1983–84)	n.a.	369
99th (1985–86)	1,074	548

SOURCES: *Congressional Record* and *Congressional Quarterly Almanac* for each year. For information on sources, methods and definitions, see Steven S. Smith, "Going to the Floor: Changing Patterns of Participation in the U.S. House of Representatives, 1955–1986," Brookings Discussion Paper in Governmental Studies no. 13 (Brookings, September 1987); and Smith, *Call to Order: Floor Politics in the House and Senate* (Brookings, forthcoming).
n.a. Not available.
a. Measures in connection with which there was at least one "key vote," as identified by *Congressional Quarterly.*

the 96th and 99th Congresses did not reflect a change in members' desires to offer floor amendments so much as a change in their opportunities to do so.

When one looks more closely at the amendments proposed and adopted on the House floor during the 91st–94th Congresses (1969–76), the data presented in table 2-4 call attention to several other respects in which the 93d Congress (1973–74) evidently marked a turning point in the amending process. Comparing the 91st and 92d Congresses with the two that followed, there was only a slight increase in the percentage of measures the House passed to which members offered one or more floor amendments. On the other hand, the number of contested amendments, those which members accepted or rejected by a three-to-two margin or less, increased by roughly 50 percent between the 92d and 93d Congresses. There were equally impressive increases as well in the number of amendments proposed per day the House was in session and in the number of amendments representatives offered per capita. Per capita amending activity increased markedly among Republicans and sophomore members, and, to a somewhat lesser extent, among Democrats and senior members as well. The percentage of amendments offered by noncommittee members did not increase, but their success rate clearly did.

TABLE 2-4. Trends in House Floor Amendments Proposed and
Adopted, 91st–94th Congresses (1969–76)

Characteristic	91st ('69–'70)	92d ('71–'72)	93d ('73–'74)	94th ('75–'76)
	Congress			
Number of amendments proposed				
Contested amendments[a]	126	152	226	232
Amendments per day in session	2.5	2.7	4.5	4.4
Amendments per capita	2.0	1.8	3.3	3.1
Per capita by Democrats	2.5	2.2	3.2	2.9
Per capita by Republicans	1.4	1.3	3.3	3.7
Per capita by sophomores[a]	1.8	1.3	3.7	2.2
Per capita by senior members[b]	2.3	2.1	3.6	3.4
Percent of measures passed that were subjected to 1 or more amendments	18.2	21.8	27.9	24.1
Percent of amendments proposed				
By noncommittee members	48.3	51.8	48.5	47.8
By Republicans	31.6	28.9	43.8	39.1
Percent of amendments adopted	45.8	47.1	52.1	54.7
Offered by noncommittee members	36.8	36.6	46.8	49.6
Offered by Democrats	48.7	50.3	59.5	61.2
Offered by Republicans	39.7	39.3	42.6	44.6
Offered by sophomores[b]	32.8	24.6	44.8	51.4
Offered by senior members[c]	54.6	52.5	54.4	57.9

SOURCES: Smith, *Call to Order;* and Smith, "Going to the Floor."
a. Accepted or rejected by a three-to-two margin or less.
b. Second-term members.
c. Members with four or more terms of service.

The winning percentages of Democratic and Republican amendments also increased, but it was the sophomore members whose collective batting average improved most dramatically.

The sheer increase in amending activity posed problems for Democratic floor managers, of course, because they had to respond to more challenges to their committees' (or subcommittees') positions. This development also created problems and uncertainties for the Speaker and his colleagues in the majority party leadership, including the Democratic members of the Rules Committee.[25] First, scheduling legislative business

25. During the 93d–97th Congresses, the effective leader of the Rules Committee was Richard Bolling, even before he officially became chairman in 1979. Bolling was particularly sensitive to the problems and perspective of the Speaker and the Democratic floor leaders.

on the floor, which is the Speaker's principal prerogative and responsibility, becomes more difficult when neither he nor a bill's floor manager can predict with confidence how long it will take to complete floor action on it. Second, delays resulting from debate and votes on unexpected amendments can affect who is on Capitol Hill and available to vote, and scheduling decisions sometimes turn on the attendance of one's allies and opponents. Third, the longer a bill remains on the floor, the greater are the dangers that external events may upset the most carefully calibrated political and policy calculations and that opponents will have enough time to mobilize opposition on key votes.

Unfortunately for the Democratic leadership, though, the surge in amending activity caused more than mere scheduling difficulties. As table 2-3 shows, the most important and controversial measures, those provoking one or more key votes, also faced an increase in amending activity. We have also shown that the number of contested amendments increased, as did the proportion of all amendments offered by members of the minority party. Even worse, at least from the perspective of the Speaker and Democratic committee chairmen, more of these amendments were more likely to win, especially on recorded votes. By the 93d and 94th Congresses, as table 2-4 indicates, the average amendment was slightly more likely to win than to lose. These developments made the House floor a more hazardous place for committees and the majority party, even though members of both also took increasing advantage of the opportunities available to them on the floor. The result was greater uncertainty about what amendments were going to be offered, when, by whom, and with what result.

Republicans were more than ready to take advantage of recorded voting in Committee of the Whole. The per capita rate of amending activity for Republicans soon exceeded the rate for Democrats, as minority party members tried to reverse losses they had suffered in committee markups or at least to cause divisions and embarrassment among Democrats. Some Republicans, including John Ashbrook, Robert Bauman, and John Rousselot, seemed to make a special effort to propose amendments that challenged committee positions. They sometimes offered amendments not with any real expectation of winning, but with the intention of delaying final passage, creating a backlog of legislation awaiting floor action, or forcing Democrats to take publicly recorded positions on controversial issues. In fact, Bauman even entertained requests from Republican congressional candidates who asked him to propose particular amendments (on federal funding for abortions, for example) that would create political difficulties for the Democratic incumbents whom they were challenging.[26]

The volume of amending activity, along with the time it consumed and the unpredictability it created, caused problems for all representatives, not just the majority party leaders. Everyone in the House found that they were being exposed to unanticipated votes that could be politically dangerous. And they also found it more difficult to schedule their own activities, congressional and personal. Long daily sessions, extended by debates and votes on what sometimes seemed to be an endless series of amendments, strained collegiality and tested members' tolerance of their colleagues' floor behavior.[27] In an August 1979 letter to the Speaker and Chairman Bolling of the Rules Committee, Democrat John LaFalce of New York and forty-two other Democrats argued that "without relief of some kind, we won't be able to do the jobs for which we were elected and the ultimate result will be inefficient Members in an inefficient institution."[28]

Perhaps most important to Democratic leaders and other members who shared their perspective, they faced more risk of losing votes on important floor amendments. In addition to the developments within the House that have been discussed, changes in the political and policy environment added to the increasingly complicated and uncertain situation faced by the Democrats' leaders, including their members on Rules. The familiar litany of political changes included the decline in Democratic party identification, Republican victories in recent presidential elections, the growing costs of congressional campaigns with the attendant pressures of fundraising, the influx of new members with less patience and prior elective experience, and the reelection advantages available to any incumbent regardless of party or position in the House. All these developments weakened the ties between congressional leaders and their followers.

Most Democratic representatives continued to vote with their party leaders most of the time, but more from calculation than from obligation. Changes in the definition of policies and the salience of issues also created new pressures within the House and its majority party—for ex-

26. Interview with Robert Bauman, July 16, 1987.
27. Daily sessions averaged an hour (roughly 20 percent) longer in the 94th–96th Congresses than in the five preceding Congresses. See Norman J. Ornstein and others, *Vital Statistics on Congress, 1982* (Washington, D.C.: American Enterprise Institute for Public Policy Research, 1982), pp. 130–31.
28. Letter dated August 2, 1979.

ample, by straining jurisdictional treaties among committees and by creating new cross-pressures and less predictable divisions within party ranks. These changes also contributed to voting alignments on the floor that were more fluid and less predictable than those in the 1950s and 1960s.[29] The freshmen classes of the early 1970s offered the Democratic leadership less reliable support, while the decline of the "Rockefeller wing" of the Republican party meant that on major issues there were fewer votes that Democratic leaders could muster from the other side of the aisle. At a time when recorded teller votes, multiple referrals, committee decentralization, and increased amending activity all had combined to make the House floor a more important and uncertain site for policymaking, the majority leadership's task of coalition building had become more difficult.

Democratic leaders responded by exploiting the rules of the House for whatever parliamentary advantages they might offer and also by changing the rules in several ways to limit the dangers they otherwise could confront on the floor. For example, Democratic chairmen arranged with the Speaker to bring more and more bills to the floor under suspension of the rules, a procedure that permits consideration of committee amendments only. At the beginning of the 93d Congress in 1973, the House amended Rule XXVII to double the number of days on which suspension motions are in order and doubled it again four years later when the 95th Congress convened. And the use of this procedure grew apace. The House considered fewer than 200 suspension motions in each of the Congresses between 1967 and 1972, but more than 400 such motions in three of the four Congresses between 1977 and 1984.[30]

At the beginning of the 96th Congress (1979), the Democratic Caucus sponsored another change in the rules, this time amending Rule XXIII to make it somewhat more difficult to secure publicly recorded votes on amendments. The amendment increased from twenty to twenty-five the number of members required to order a recorded vote in Committee of the Whole. Then, four years later when the 98th Congress convened, the caucus secured an imaginative amendment to Rule XXI, the effect of which was to permit a simple majority of members to cast an ostensibly "procedural" vote in Committee of the Whole to protect themselves against having to consider limitation amendments to a general appropria-

29. Barbara Sinclair, "Coping with Uncertainty: Building Coalitions in the House and the Senate," in Mann and Ornstein, eds., *The New Congress*, pp. 178–220.

30. Stanley Bach, "Suspension of the Rules in the House of Representatives," report 86-103 GOV (Congressional Research Service, May 12, 1986), p. 62.

tions bill.[31] Such amendments had been the most readily available and effective means for members, especially Republicans, to compel the House to vote on controversial issues, such as abortion and busing, that the standing committees had not brought to the floor as freestanding bills.[32]

Changing the standing rules, however, was a relatively inflexible way to cope with the uncertainties Democratic leaders and their allies now confronted on the floor. The special rules reported by the Rules Committee were a far more flexible device that could be adapted to suit the political and procedural circumstances accompanying each bill. The committee had begun to experiment with a few "restrictive" rules, largely at the urging of Richard Bolling and fellow Rules Democrat Gillis Long of Louisiana.[33] Now more and more Democrats were beginning to recognize the utility of such rules and to encourage their use. So LaFalce and his colleagues wrote Bolling and the Speaker in 1979 to ask for a "judicious expansion" of the use of special rules limiting floor amendments, arguing that, for purposes of both political and institutional management, the Rules Committee should assert more active and discriminating control over the amendment process on the House floor.[34]

A Changing Rules Committee

The House's Democratic leaders and their followers would not even have considered turning to the Rules Committee to help them cope with the

31. The vote occurs on a nondebatable motion that the Committee of the Whole rise and report the measure, as amended to that point, back to the House for final passage. Adoption of this motion precludes consideration of limitation amendments.

32. There also were bipartisan complaints among members about the sheer volume of roll call votes and the ways in which such frequent votes consumed their time and disrupted their schedules. In response, the House made several other changes in its rules and practices, sometimes in the face of Republican opposition, to eliminate opportunities for procedural votes. The Rules Committee also changed the standard terms of special rules to eliminate the need for a motion (and, therefore, a vote) on resolving into Committee of the Whole. And the Speaker was given authority to postpone and cluster a series of roll call votes, an authority exercised most often during consideration of suspension motions.

33. See Bruce I. Oppenheimer, "The Changing Relationship Between House Leadership and the Committee on Rules," in Frank H. Mackaman, ed., *Understanding Congressional Leadership* (Washington, D.C.: Congressional Quarterly Press, 1981), pp. 218–22.

34. Robert Bauman argued that "some embarrassing Democratic leadership setbacks on key Republican floor amendments" provoked the LaFalce letter, "beseeching them [O'Neill and Bolling] to save Democrats from themselves. . . ." Robert E. Bauman, "Majority Tyranny in the House," in John H. Rousselot and Richard T. Schulze, eds., *View From the Capitol Dome (Looking Right)* (Ottawa, Ill.: Green Hill Publishers, 1980), p. 11.

developments we have cataloged had it not been for the 1961 vote that increased the size of the committee and began to break the hold of its conservative coalition.[35] Then, during the first half of the 1970s, the Democratic Caucus made two changes in its rules that tied the committee's Democrats still more closely to their party colleagues in general and to the Speaker in particular.

First, the caucus adopted a rule in 1973 requiring advance public notice whenever a committee chairman requests that the Rules Committee grant a special rule that would limit or prohibit germane floor amendments. The caucus also established a procedure for calling a meeting at which its members could vote to instruct the Democratic members of Rules to support a rule permitting certain amendments to be considered on the floor. Aimed primarily at the closed rules the Ways and Means Committee had become accustomed to receiving, the 1973 rules change was provoked primarily by controversy over the oil depletion allowance. The caucus rarely has seen fit to instruct its members on Rules since then. But it did send a signal to Democrats on all House legislative committees, including Ways and Means and Rules, that they should pay more attention to the policy preferences and procedural interests of the rank-and-file membership of the caucus, who no longer could be counted on to accept closed rules.

Second, just before the start of the 94th Congress (1975-76), the caucus strengthened the linkage between the Rules Committee and the Democratic leadership by adopting a resolution, sponsored by Bolling, to give the Speaker direct authority to nominate all Democratic members of Rules, subject to caucus approval, while leaving Democratic nominations to other standing committees in the hands of the party's Steering and Policy Committee. The caucus rule also made explicit that the Speaker's authority extended to renominations of Democrats already serving on Rules. These special arrangements made it clear that the Rules Committee occupied a unique position between the majority party and the House. They also gave the Speaker greater leverage over Rules members and their decisions and firmly established the principle that the commit-

---

35. On the 1961 affair, its origins, and aftermath, see Milton C. Cummings, Jr., and Robert L. Peabody, "The Decision to Enlarge the Committee on Rules: An Analysis of the 1961 Vote," and Peabody, "The Enlarged Rules Committee," both in Robert L. Peabody and Nelson W. Polsby, eds., *New Perspectives on the House of Representatives* (Rand McNally, 1963), pp. 129–94. See also the sources cited in note 8 of chap. 1; Richard Bolling, *House Out of Order* (E.P. Dutton, 1965), pp. 195–220; and Neil MacNeil, *Forge of Democracy: The House of Representatives* (David McKay, 1963), pp. 410–48.

tee was to be responsive to the wishes of the majority party as expressed by its leadership. Rules became known to some as the "Speaker's committee," reflecting the influence the Speaker could exercise over its decisions.[36]

As Speakers, both John McCormack and Carl Albert had promoted the assignment of more loyal and liberal Democrats to Rules in the 1960s and early 1970s. At Albert's behest, for instance, the Democratic Caucus took the unusual step of filling one of the three vacancies on the committee in 1973 with a freshman—Clem Rogers McSpadden, from the Speaker's home state of Oklahoma. Albert also chose Gillis Long, who would prove to be a valuable lieutenant of the party leadership, over Sonny Montgomery of Mississippi, the candidate of most southern conservatives. The Speaker's new appointment power then enabled Albert and his successor, Tip O'Neill, to accelerate the trend. In 1975, Joe Moakley of Massachusetts and Andrew Young of Georgia were appointed to the committee, and they were followed in 1979 by Shirley Chisholm, Christopher Dodd, and Lloyd Meeds—all from the liberal wing of the party. Responding to criticism from conservative Democrats, O'Neill subsequently appointed more moderate Democrats, but the ideological flavor of the majority party contingent on Rules had been altered for many years to come.

Had the Rules Committee become a mere errand boy for the Speaker, receiving his instructions and doing his bidding, the Speaker would have had to confront most of the growing hazards and uncertainties of House politics. But throughout the 1970s and into the present decade, Albert and O'Neill took a direct interest only in special rules for considering

36. See Oppenheimer, "The Rules Committee." Oppenheimer notes a decline between the 88th–90th (1963–68) and the 91st–93d (1969–74) Congresses in the number of requested rules that the Rules Committee failed to grant and takes this as evidence of the committee's increased responsiveness to the will of the majority party and its leadership (pp. 99–102). Since then the number of rules not granted has moved back toward the earlier, higher levels. Readers interested in the pattern of rules not granted may write the authors for a table summarizing their data. We believe that the political meaning of changes in the numbers of rules not granted cannot readily be determined from the data themselves, so we have chosen not to give them much emphasis. For instance, the unusually large number of bills on which the committee failed to hold a hearing during the 96th Congress, when Bolling first became its chairman, may have been a deliberate signal to the other standing committees to be more responsive to party leadership preferences by being more discriminating in the legislation they sought to bring to the floor. More generally, refusals to grant rules can also reflect unresolved intercommittee disputes, late-session scheduling constraints, and other problems that do not represent the exercise of political discretion by the Rules Committee. Nevertheless, there certainly have been cases, such as recent banking reform legislation, in which Rules delayed or denied rules, seemingly at its own discretion and sometimes because of the intense concerns of one or more of its Democratic members.

truly important legislation. Rules members acted fairly independently on legislation of only moderate controversy and party interest.[37] And in turn, the prominence and prestige of some Rules Democrats were enhanced by their role as intermediaries among the standing committees, their bill managers, the Speaker, and the rank-and-file membership of the House.[38] Indeed, the two Speakers seemed to appreciate the value of the Rules Committee as a buffer to absorb both shocks and blame. Nor was there often a compelling need for the Speaker to become involved personally; he usually could depend on Rules Committee Democrats to protect his interests, which frequently did not extend far beyond passing bills that satisfied the committees of jurisdiction without dividing Democratic ranks on the floor. And he also could depend on Richard Bolling.

First as the de facto Rules chairman and then as de jure chairman in the 96th and 97th Congresses (1979–82), Bolling assumed personal responsibility for drafting most of the special rules that were likely to provoke controversy. His Democratic colleagues on the committee usually deferred to his judgment, both because of his long-time relationship with the Speaker and because of his unquestioned mastery of legislative procedure. "My technique," Bolling explained, "was to take the responsibility and to take my lumps when things went wrong."[39] Thus Bolling played a key role in adjusting special rules to the circumstances of the late 1970s and early 1980s. In devising special rules, he was an innovator who urged bill managers and other friendly legislators to request rules suited to their needs. As we shall discuss in the following chapter, one of Bolling's primary legacies was the tactical design of special rules to respond to the set of problems and opportunities accompanying each major bill, rather than merely selecting from among a handful of standard forms.

During Bolling's tenure, he frequently would draft a rule and present it at a meeting of Rules Democrats before the committee's formal hearing. One observer characterized Bolling's influence with telling overstatement: "He would tell O'Neill what he thought was needed, and then he would tell [Rules Democratic] members that was what O'Neill wanted. He scripted the whole thing."[40] Claude Pepper, who became chairman of

37. These observations about the Rules Committee during the Albert and O'Neill speakerships are based in part on interviews with former Chairman Richard Bolling and with other Democratic members of Rules and senior aides to the Speaker, the committee, and its members.

38. See, for example, Oppenheimer, "The Rules Committee"; and Andy Plattner, "Controlling the Floor: Rules Under Chairman Pepper Looks Out for the Democrats," *Congressional Quarterly Weekly Report*, vol. 43 (August 24, 1985), pp. 1671–75.

39. Interview with Richard Bolling, October 24, 1986.

40. Plattner, "Controlling the Floor," p. 1674.

the committee in 1983, usually was not as assertive as Bolling had been, but others, such as Gillis Long and Joe Moakley, took up some of the slack. Democratic committee members continued to caucus in advance, but they tended to share responsibility for designing rules as part of a more collective enterprise, one in which they normally developed a consensus on the appropriate rule. What remained unchanged under Pepper was the committee's substantial independence. Pepper explained, "Ninety-nine percent of the time, the Speaker never communicates at all." Anthony Beilenson, one of Pepper's Democratic colleagues on the committee, elaborated: "The Speaker does not ask much of us, partly because we mostly do what we think he wants."[41]

Relations between Rules Democrats and the Speaker changed considerably soon after Jim Wright was elected Speaker at the beginning of the 100th Congress in 1987. Wright, who was anxious to establish a strong legislative record and begin to define himself as Speaker, intervened directly to decide the terms of special rules for major legislation he rushed to the floor early in 1987. Wright *was* asking much of the Rules Committee, to the consternation of some committee Democrats. Later in the 100th Congress, he loosened his grip over rules as measures less vital to his agenda came to the floor. But he clearly established that special rules would be tools of the leadership and that the Speaker would insist they remain well oiled and ready for use.

41. Ibid. We shall return to this subject in chap. 5.

CHAPTER THREE

Change and Creativity in Capitol Suite H313

MEMBERS OF THE Rules Committee have responded to the changing conditions in the House—including the changing demands made on them by party leaders, committee and subcommittee chairmen, and rank-and-file members of both parties—by adaptations in the special rules they have recommended to the House. As we noted in chapter 1, most of these rules have two essential purposes. First, they recommend a measure for floor consideration. Second, they propose a set of procedures, which both supplement and supplant the House's standing rules, to govern consideration of that measure, especially the amending process in Committee of the Whole. We turn now to an examination of the special rules the Rules Committee granted and the House adopted during the 94th–99th Congresses (1975–86). This period witnessed a transformation in the design of these resolutions. By crafting special rules in innovative and increasingly diverse ways, the Rules Committee assisted Democratic bill managers and party leaders, and often the House as a whole, to manage the more uncertain, complex, and conflict-ridden conditions the House came to face in making its legislative decisions.

"An Original Bill for the Purpose of Amendment"

When the House resolves into Committee of the Whole to consider a measure, members proceed to debate and offer amendments to its text in the form in which it had been introduced and referred to committee, unless the special rule governing this process directs otherwise. And, in fact, special rules frequently provide for the House to take up a particular bill, but then specify some other text that is to be the focus of debate and amendment. This type of rule redirects members' attention, and their amendments, to a proposed new version of the bill's text—a version that may be significantly, even radically, different from its original text. For example, after a standing committee finishes marking up a measure that had been referred to it, it often orders that bill reported back to the House with a single amendment that consolidates all of the discrete changes the committee approved. This "amendment in the nature of a substitute," as it is known to the House, proposes to "strike out all after the enacting [or resolving] clause and insert in lieu thereof" a new text, which constitutes the committee's recommendations for legislation.

In such cases, the standing committee, the Rules Committee, and the House as a whole invariably agree that members will be concerned primarily with the committee's proposed substitute during the amending process in Committee of the Whole. The committee substitute is presumed to be preferable to the original version of the bill because the substitute represents the informed, expert judgment of the committee, and members know from experience that there is virtually no doubt this substitute ultimately will be adopted to replace the text of the bill as introduced. Therefore they have every incentive to propose their amendments to the substitute, knowing that it is this version of the bill the House is nearly certain to pass. Like other amendments, however, the committee substitute is a first-degree amendment that is amendable on the floor in only one further degree; by contrast, members may amend the text of a measure itself in two degrees. Under these circumstances, when a standing committee reports a bill with an amendment in the nature of a substitute, the special rule for considering that bill typically permits members to amend the substitute on the floor in two degrees, by providing that the committee version be considered "as an original bill for the purpose of amendment under the five-minute rule."[1]

Table 3-1 documents the changes that have occurred since the mid-1970s in the provisions of special rules governing the legislative texts to be debated and amended. Only about half the special rules adopted in recent Congresses (compared with two-thirds of the rules in the 94th

1. A standing committee can recommend a complete new legislative text by reporting it as an amendment in the nature of a substitute for the text of a bill that had been referred to the committee, or by reporting it as the text of a new "clean" bill that the committee authorizes its chairman to introduce and report on its behalf. The text of a clean bill, like that of any other measure, is amendable in two degrees on the House floor. Thus, by providing for a committee substitute to be considered as "an original bill," the Rules Committee proposes that members have the same opportunities to amend the committee's position that they would have had if the committee had reported a clean bill instead. To the same end, the Rules Committee includes two other compensating changes in the text of any special rule that makes a different text in order "as an original bill." These changes protect members' rights to demand separate votes in the House on amendments adopted in Committee of the Whole and to offer motions to recommit with instructions.

TABLE 3-1. Frequency of Provisions Governing the Text to Be
Amended, 94th–99th Congresses (1975–86)
Percent

| | Congress | | | | | |
Type of measure	94th ('75–'76)	95th ('77–'78)	96th ('79–'80)	97th ('81–'82)	98th ('83–'84)	99th ('85–'86)
Single-committee measures						
Measure as introduced	68.6	64.3	67.3	56.3	58.4	55.0
Committee substitute	30.5	35.1	31.4	38.8	36.6	40.0
Alternative substitute	0.9	0.6	1.3	5.0	5.0	5.0
N	223	154	156	80	101	80
Multiple-committee measures						
Measure as introduced	47.1	43.3	39.1	35.0	27.3	40.0
Committee substitute	52.9	40.0	43.5	40.0	31.8	25.0
Alternative substitute	0	16.7	17.4	25.0	40.9	35.0
N	17	30	23	20	22	20
All measures[a]						
Measure as introduced	68.1	61.3	64.1	53.8	53.6	52.5
Committee substitute	31.0	35.5	32.6	37.5	35.2	36.6
Alternative substitute	0.8	3.2	3.3	8.7	11.2	10.9
N	248	186	181	104	125	101

SOURCES: Final *Calendars* of the House of Representatives and the Committee on Rules.
a. Includes measures that were not referred to or reported from a committee.

Congress) have directed amendments to the original texts of bills reported by one or more of the House's standing committees, including the
texts of "clean bills" introduced after markup by chairmen on behalf of
their committees. With increased frequency, a substitute text of some
kind has been designated as the vehicle for amending activity on the
House floor. In part, this reflects the popularity of committee substitutes
since at least the mid-1960s.[2] This type of substitute rule has become a

2. Stanley Bach, "Special Rules in the House of Representatives: Themes and Contemporary Variations," *Congressional Studies,* vol. 8, no. 2 (1981), pp. 43–48. House committees
may be somewhat more inclined to favor amendments in the nature of substitutes, rather
than clean bills, when reporting longer, more important, and more controversial bills. These
also are the bills that are most likely to generate widespread public interest and organized
campaigns of support and opposition. By reporting such a measure with a committee substitute—and thereby preserving the number of the bill or resolution as it was originally introduced, even while proposing to entirely replace its text—rather than a clean bill with a

familiar and routine device for dealing with committee proposals, and it rarely provokes anything more than a brief mention on the House floor.

Of greater interest is a more recent phenomenon: the appearance of special rules in which the Rules Committee has directed floor debate and amendments to an "alternative substitute" that has not been approved by vote of any of the House's standing committees. In recent Congresses, as table 3-1 reveals, the committee has proposed, in an increasing number and proportion of cases, that an amendment in the nature of a substitute, but not a committee substitute, be considered as the original bill for purposes of amendment. Such an alternative substitute replaces both the text of the bill as introduced and the amendments to it proposed by the committee or committees to which the bill had been referred. This new version typically is devised after the committee (or committees) has reported the bill that the rule would make in order, and it usually is identified as the text of another measure or as an amendment that has been printed for the information of the House in the Rules Committee's report or in the *Congressional Record*.

Although the use of alternative substitutes still is exceptional, it has become an available and recognized option for which members must be alert. The emergence of rules providing for alternative substitutes has been one response by the standing committees, in cooperation with the Rules Committee, to the potential difficulties and conflicts engendered by multiple referrals.[3] Roughly two-thirds of these rules adopted during 1975–86 were for consideration of measures that had been referred to more than one committee; during this same period, less than one-fifth of all special rules adopted were for considering multiple-committee bills.[4]

---

different number, the committee can avoid confusing and disrupting the "grassroots" lobbying campaign from which it expects to benefit.

3. See Roger H. Davidson and Walter J. Oleszek, "From Monopoly to Interaction: Changing Patterns of Committee Management of Legislation in the House," paper prepared for the 1987 annual meeting of the Midwest Political Science Association, pp. 31–32.

4. On occasion, the Rules Committee has reported an alternative substitute rule for considering a single-committee bill, sometimes in order to avoid a need for the reporting committee to meet again to vote formally for a committee substitute. After reporting a bill, for example, a committee may learn that its proposal could provoke a jurisdictional problem for another committee, perhaps leading to open conflict on the floor or a request for a sequential referral. See, for example, H. Res. 536, for consideration of H.R. 2482, the Federal Insecticide, Fungicide, and Rodenticide Act Amendments of 1986, *Congressional Record*, daily edition (September 17, 1986), pp. H7043–46. Or the reporting committee may become concerned about a potential point of order under the Budget Act against its bill and find it preferable to cure the violation rather than request a waiver from the Rules Committee. See, for example, H. Res. 402, for consideration of H.R. 4151, the Omnibus Diplomatic Security and Anti-Terrorism Act, *Congressional Record*, daily edition (March 18, 1986),

And as table 3-1 indicates, alternative substitute rules have become as common as any other device for structuring floor consideration of multiple-committee measures.

These trends suggest that since the mid-1970s House committees sharing jurisdiction over bills have been increasingly interested and successful in avoiding open intercommittee conflict on the floor. When two or more committees report conflicting or inconsistent amendments to the same bill, their leaders may meet unofficially to devise a compromise version acceptable to the committees' majority party members. They then request that the Rules Committee make this compromise alternative substitute in order as the focus of debate and amendment, rather than the original version of the bill or any of the amendments formally approved by the committees.

Consider the special rule, H. Res. 331, that Rules Chairman Claude Pepper brought to the floor in early December 1985, for the Superfund Amendments of 1985 (H.R. 2817), a complex and controversial bill relating to chemical wastes and other environmental problems. After allocating the time for general debate among five standing committees, the resolution provided that "it shall be in order to consider an amendment in the nature of a substitute consisting of the text of the bill H.R. 3852 as an original bill for the purpose of amendment under the five-minute rule. . . ." This alternative substitute was a compromise between Chairmen John Dingell of the Committee on Energy and Commerce and James Howard of the Committee on Public Works and Transportation, their ranking minority members, and leaders of the other three committees with a jurisdictional interest in the bill; the two party floor leaders also had joined in sponsoring it. Everyone, including Pepper, commended everyone else:

> We in the Rules Committee know how complex this problem is and if we had been faced with a bitter dispute or sharp difference of opinion between those two important committees, it would have been extremely difficult for the Rules Committee, and I think it would have been extremely difficult for the House to have determined what is the right course in the public interest for us to pursue.
>
> Now by the kindness and the diligent and dedicated work of

---

pp. H1231–33. In such cases, the committee's chairman can avoid such problems and expedite the bill's floor consideration by preparing an amendment that Rules makes in order as an alternative substitute.

these two great committee chairmen and their colleagues and associates, we are presented with a unified bill produced by those two
important committees, Energy and Commerce and Public Works
and Transportation.[5]

As this statement suggests, the Rules Committee and especially its
Democratic members almost always welcome such alternative substitutes. The resulting floor situation is less complicated and confusing than
it would be if members had to cast a series of floor votes to choose between the committees' positions. Also, any rule arranging for such votes
could be perceived as giving one of the committees a procedural advantage, and Rules generally has no interest in putting itself in the middle
of fights between other standing committees. As one of the committee's
senior Republican staff assistants put it in a recent interview, "The Rules
Committee does not want to be in a position of favoring one committee
over another in structuring a rule."[6]

One of the most striking examples of how the Rules Committee may
have to respond to intercommittee disagreements arose in 1979, when
there were three competing versions of an Alaska lands bill, each of which
enjoyed significant support among one or more of the committees of jurisdiction. When no compromise could be reached, the Rules Committee
proposed a rule that selected one version to be the original bill for purposes of amendment, a second to be a substitute for the first, and the
third to be a substitute for the second, so that both the second and third
versions also were perfectible by second-degree amendments. Although
Rules Committee members argued they had no such intention, others
claimed that this arrangement favored the third substitute (which would
be voted on first). Such complaints probably would have been unavoid-
able no matter what sequence the committee had proposed for members
to vote on the three versions, which is precisely why Rules members
prefer to avoid being put in such situations.[7]

In a more recent case of competing committee proposals, the Judiciary
Committee sought in 1984 to strike provisions from each of the two titles

5. *Congressional Record* (December 5, 1985), pp. 34505–10.

6. On the other hand, the threat of a rule favoring one committee over another, or
merely the perception that such a result is possible, can be a powerful incentive for the
potentially disadvantaged committee to negotiate a compromise.

7. On this episode, see Stanley Bach, "The Structure of Choice in the House of Representatives: The Impact of Complex Special Rules," *Harvard Journal on Legislation*, vol. 18
(Summer 1981), pp. 591–93.

of an Energy and Commerce Committee substitute for a bill dealing with drug approvals and patents. The special rule (H. Res. 569) designated the Energy and Commerce version as the text to be amended and then made the Judiciary Committee amendments in order, en bloc, to each of its titles. Without this provision, the Judiciary Committee's amendments would have been in order anyway (they needed no waivers of points of order), and they still would have enjoyed precedence over any other amendments to each title. But the Judiciary amendments would have been considered one at a time, not en bloc. The effect of H. Res. 569 was to protect Judiciary against having to present its proposals in a piecemeal fashion and to allow members to make a clear choice (by their votes on the Judiciary Committee amendments) between the two committees' positions on each title.[8]

In addition to its institutional interest in avoiding the need to create such complicated and potentially contentious situations, the Democratic majority on Rules also has a political interest in avoiding open disagreements on the floor among Democratic committee leaders. Public divisions within the majority party reduce the probability of success on the floor; they also can embarrass party leaders on visible issues and create interpersonal frictions that may spill over to other legislation. As a result, Rules Committee Democrats have encouraged the development of intercommittee compromise substitutes and sometimes have even insisted that committees work out their differences before Rules will consider granting their bill a special rule. In turn, as committee and subcommittee leaders have become more familiar with the advantages of this procedure and its appeal to the Rules Committee, they also have become more likely to adopt it at their own initiative.

Republican members of Rules have reason to support alternative substitute rules when intercommittee disputes involve conflicts among ranking minority members as well as chairmen and when senior committee Republicans are included in the negotiations, as in the case of the Superfund rule. But the development of these substitutes frequently excludes committee Republicans and can reverse victories the minority won during committee markup. In addition, special rules making compromise substitutes in order as original text can put committee Republicans and all other members at a significant disadvantage on the floor vis-à-vis the committee members who developed the substitute. In such cases, there is no committee report explaining the text to be considered, nor is there the three-day layover period that normally gives members some minimal time to

8. *Congressional Record*, daily edition (August 8, 1984), pp. H8701–05.

assess it and develop their amendments.[9] Furthermore, while public disagreement between or among committees may encourage members to propose their own preferences as floor amendments, members may be less willing to do so when confronted with an agreement supported by majorities on both or all the committees of jurisdiction.[10] Thus, whether intentionally or not, this technique for resolving intercommittee differences probably makes the resulting compromise substitute more resistant to successful challenges on the floor.

Advance Notice of Amendments

Without otherwise restricting floor amendments, the Rules Committee sometimes has required that they must be printed in advance in the *Congressional Record* if they are to be in order on the floor.[11] Members may offer whatever proper amendments they wish, but they must give advance written notice of their intentions and the precise terms of their proposals. This practice also began during the 1970s, and while relatively few special rules have included such advance notice requirements, they presaged the more severe restrictions on amendments that would follow

9. The only protection is the provision of clause 4(b) of Rule XI that the House usually may not consider a special rule on the same legislative day it is reported, except by a two-thirds vote. This clause was at the center of contention on the floor on October 29, 1987, when the House rejected a special rule for considering an omnibus budget reconciliation bill and then agreed to Majority Leader Thomas Foley's motion that the House adjourn momentarily in the middle of the day. Foley made this motion to create a second legislative day on the same calendar day in order to permit the Rules Committee to call up another special rule without the need for a two-thirds vote. On this incident, see *Congressional Record*, daily edition (October 29, 1987), pp. H9155–66.

10. In this regard, Fleisher and Bond conclude from their analysis of voting on House and Senate floor amendments that "if committee members are highly unified for or against an amendment, the committee position is almost certain to prevail." Richard Fleisher and Jon R. Bond, "Beyond Committee Control: Committee and Party Leader Influence on Floor Amendments in Congress," *American Politics Quarterly*, vol. 11 (April 1983), pp. 131–61.

11. In the absence of such a requirement, members sometimes submit their amendments for printing in the *Record* to gain the protection of clause 6 of Rule XXIII (*House Rules and Manual*, pp. 620–23). This clause provides that, even when the time for debating amendments to a bill in Committee of the Whole has expired, after having been limited by majority vote or unanimous consent, there shall be ten minutes for debating each amendment printed in the *Record* after the bill was reported but at least one day before being offered. This protection can be valuable in the case, for example, of an amendment to be offered to the last title of a major bill on which members are anxious to complete action. Members also may submit amendments for printing in the *Record* in order to inform the bill managers (and others) of their intentions and perhaps to stimulate negotiations toward a mutually acceptable compromise.

(see table 3-5 below).[12] Like the use of alternative substitutes, the requirement for advance notice of amendments is another device by which the Rules Committee has adapted its special rules to protect House committees and subcommittees—and often the majority party leadership of the House—against the dangers and uncertainties of floor amendments.

One set of arguments frequently made in support of barring all floor amendments is that legislating by amendment on the floor is unwise when the subject of the bill is technical, its provisions are complex and carefully balanced, and the effect of amendments cannot be fully analyzed and evaluated while they are being debated under the five-minute rule. The advance notice requirement developed as a way of responding to these concerns without denying members the opportunity to propose their amendments. By requiring that amendments be printed in the *Record* some time before being offered, such special rules give bill managers, other committee members, and the committee staff an opportunity to study the amendments' implications in advance. In this way, the House can continue to benefit from the experience and expertise of its committees without being limited simply to voting for or against the bills they report. The result, so the argument goes, is a legislative process that is both open and responsible.

On September 20, 1985, for example, the House took up H. Res. 267, the rule for considering H.R. 2100, the Food Security Act of 1985, an omnibus farm bill of major importance. In what was quite a complicated rule, most members were affected primarily by the prohibition against floor amendments "except amendments printed in the *Congressional Record* on or before September 24, 1985." Speaking for the Democratic majority on Rules, David Bonior of Michigan noted that the bill contained new spending authority, contract authority, target prices, price supports, and farm credit programs. Therefore, Bonior argued, the advance notice requirement "was necessary to expedite consideration of this complex legislation as well as to facilitate the evaluation of each amendment's potential budgetary impact."[13] No one disagreed. The bill did involve a variety of complicated and expensive programs, and members were given

12. When the Rules Committee grants a special rule making only certain amendments in order, it often has identified each of them by reference to its sponsor and the issue of the *Congressional Record* in which the amendment is printed: for example, "an amendment printed in the Congressional Record of October 17, 1985, by, and if offered by, Representative Latta of Ohio." *Congressional Record* (October 23, 1985), p. 28607. More recently the committee has begun instead to print the full text of the amendments in the committee report accompanying the rule itself, in order to avoid any uncertainty or misunderstanding about precisely what amendments it proposes to make in order.

13. *Congressional Record* (September 20, 1985), pp. 24521–30.

four days in which to file their amendments. So they accepted the proposed rule as a reasonable restriction on their rights.

The advance notice requirement also has other advantages that members are less likely to articulate on the floor and that were not apparent during debate on the special rule for the farm bill. Giving a prospective bill manager advance warning of the amendments he may confront also gives him time to dissuade members from offering them, to negotiate compromises when possible, or to prepare arguments, mobilize opposition, and draft second-degree amendments when necessary. If floor managers in the contemporary House tend to be less experienced on the floor and less expert about the bills they bring to the floor, these advantages of the advance notice requirement can be attractive indeed. Even some Democrats on the Rules Committee, including Joe Moakley of Massachusetts, believe that there can be too much of a good, or at least useful, thing:

> Moakley is particularly irritated with the growing number of committee chairmen asking Rules to require all amendments to be submitted in advance and printed in the *Congressional Record*. Such requests are often made on the grounds that it allows more thoughtful consideration of complex amendments.
>
> But Moakley chalks it up, in part, to the inexperience of subcommittee chairmen, who increasingly are relatively junior members.
>
> "Newer chairmen are kind of unsure of themselves," said Moakley. "They ask for amendments to be printed so they can be ready for anything." [14]

On balance, though, advance notice requirements serve the interests of Democratic party leaders as well, both because they usually want to see their bill managers in firm control of floor proceedings, and because advance notice assists the leaders in planning the floor schedule by giving them some idea, however approximate and imperfect, of how much time the amending process will consume. As an assistant to Speaker O'Neill explained, all members benefit: "Members appreciate having a theater program which tells them what to expect and when to expect it." [15]

Like the use of alternative substitutes, the advantages of the advance notice requirement for committee and party leaders have corresponding

14. Janet Hook, "GOP Chafes Under Restrictive House Rules," *Congressional Quarterly Weekly Report*, vol. 45 (October 10, 1987), p. 2452.

15. Interview on November 3, 1986, with Jack Lew, formerly on the staff of the Democratic Steering and Policy Committee.

disadvantages for rank-and-file members of both parties, particularly for members who do not serve on the reporting committee. First, this requirement may reduce the number of amendments members offer by reducing the time they have to draft them, especially when the deadline for submitting amendments for printing is the same day on which the House adopts the special rule imposing the requirement. As we observed in a different context in chapter 2, members often do not focus on a bill from some other committee until the House takes up the rule for considering it; by then, it may be too late to weigh and draft amendments in time to meet the printing deadline.[16]

There even have been instances in which special rules made in order only those amendments that had been submitted for printing before the rule itself was adopted. H. Res. 578, for considering the American Defense Education Act (H.R. 5609), was such a rule. Adopted on September 13, 1984, the rule permitted members to offer only germane amendments that had been printed in the *Congressional Record* by the previous day. Speaking for the majority on Rules, David Bonior observed that adjournment was approaching and that "it is not unusual at all for the Rules Committee to develop techniques, strategies and procedures, to have this body in an orderly and expeditious way consider the legislation which is pending before the finish of this Congress." He also reminded members that they had been told the day before about the advance notice provision of this rule and had been given until 9:00 P.M. to file their amendments. But Republican Delbert Latta, also of the Rules Committee, responded that "there are probably Members who are just now becoming aware of this restriction on amendments, and it is now too late for them to prepare an amendment." More generally, Latta worried that this advance notice requirement "establishes a practice which, if followed on this type bill in the future, could prove harmful to Members on both sides of the aisle." "Sometimes debate on a bill may produce new ideas," he argued, "but under this rule, the House will be cut off from considering these new ideas because they were not submitted for printing in the *Congressional Record* yesterday." Bonior's position prevailed by more than a three-to-one margin.[17]

16. On the other hand, some observers suggest that advance notice requirements sometimes provoke an unanticipated proliferation of amendments. According to the Republican Whip, Trent Lott, "When you see you are fixin' to be cut off and not be able to have an opportunity to offer an amendment you start conjuring up all possible amendments and you put them in the Record." Hook, "GOP Chafes Under Restrictive House Rules," p. 2452. It remains to be determined, however, how many of these amendments members actually offer once they have protected their opportunity to do so.

17. *Congressional Record*, daily edition (September 13, 1984), pp. H9486–91.

Latta undoubtedly was correct that the advance notice requirement, whatever its virtues, can reduce the flexibility of the amending process. The practical effect is to limit amendments to a series of first-degree amendments that can be perfected on the floor only by unanimous consent, except for committee amendments, which normally are exempted from the requirement.[18] In return for the advance warning they receive, majority bill managers usually sacrifice the ability they normally would have to respond to unexpected tactical situations on the floor by devising their own second-degree amendments while the debate is in progress. But it is the minority party that has been most critical of advance notice requirements and their consequences. One Republican, Robert Daniel, Jr., of Virginia, made the following statement during debate on H. Res. 799, providing for consideration of H.R. 8410, the Labor Reform Act of 1977:

> I urge my colleagues to overturn this restrictive debate rule. It allows only a limited number of amendments to be offered, requiring that all potential floor amendments be printed in the *Congressional Record* in advance of the debate—which obviously does not allow any flexibility for adapting to the parliamentary situation on the floor at any given time—and allowing the leadership to throw out even amendments to the National Labor Relations Act itself on strict "nongermaneness" grounds. As a result, we will not have, if this rule for debate is railroaded through, an open forum for discussing comprehensive, well-rounded labor law reform.[19]

On behalf of the Republican contingent on Rules, John Anderson characterized the same rule as a "blitzkrieg," but Democrat Clifford Allen of Tennessee responded by noting that "there are pending now in the record over 170 amendments to almost every word, comma, and semicolon to be found in this bill." If so, the advance notice requirement hardly seems to have been particularly onerous in this case. And what Anderson sought to propose instead was not an open rule, but one that made in order a Republican substitute, or any portion of it, "without the intervention of any point of order." H.R. 8410 evidently had been drafted in such a way that the minority's policy alternative would not have been a germane amendment to it. In effect, the Republicans criticized the committee's proposed rule because it permitted only germane amendments that met the ad-

18. To benefit from this exemption, amendments typically must be offered by direction of the committee, not merely at the initiative of the committee chairman.

19. *Congressional Record* (October 4, 1977), p. 32108.

vance notice requirement and failed to provide a special exemption from the germaneness requirement for the Republican alternative.[20]

These, then, are two procedural devices that the Rules Committee has added to its options for devising special rules to help committee and party leaders cope with some of the problems they now confront on the floor. By making alternative substitutes in order as original text, for instance, the committee can accommodate the results of informal negotiations among committees to reconcile policy differences arising out of multiple referrals. And by requiring that floor amendments be printed in advance in the *Congressional Record*, special rules can assist majority floor managers in discouraging or preparing for amendments challenging their positions. But however useful (and sometimes controversial) these special rules may be, they pale in comparison with the importance of rules that protect against the dangers of the floor more directly by restricting the amendments that members may offer.

Restricting Floor Amendments

In the mid-1970s the overwhelming majority of special rules granted by the Rules Committee and adopted by the House were "open" rules that permitted members to propose the amendments of their choice, so long as their amendments met the normal requirements of House procedure, especially the germaneness rule.[21] As table 3-2 indicates, 81 percent of the rules the House adopted during the 94th Congress (1975–76) were such open rules.[22] During the 98th and 99th Congresses, by contrast, the

20. Ibid., pp. 32107–18.

21. Some open rules provide for a committee amendment in the nature of a substitute to be read as an original bill for purposes of amendment or give the same standing to an alternative substitute, as we discussed earlier in this chapter. But such provisions by themselves do not diminish members' rights to offer their own floor amendments.

22. The data presented in table 3-2 and discussed here refer to the special rules that the House adopted for initial floor consideration of measures, whether in the House, in Committee of the Whole, or in the House as in Committee of the Whole. Excluded are special rules to waive points of order, to govern further consideration of measures, or to provide for floor action on conference reports or Senate amendments, as well as a handful of rules for other, more unusual purposes. Also excluded are rules that were reported but not considered, or reported and then rejected, referred, or amended after the previous question was not ordered, and, for some purposes, rules that did not provide for general debate on measures for which there was no committee report. This discussion complements analyses of the same subject in Bach, "Special Rules in the House of Representatives," and "The Structure of Choice in the House of Representatives," which focused exclusively on special rules governing deliberations in Committee of the Whole. This study has a somewhat broader focus, which accounts for most of the differences in the data on the same Congresses presented there and here.

TABLE 3-2. Frequency of Provisions Governing Amendments, 94th–99th Congresses (1975–86)

Percent

Type of measure and rule[a]	Congress					
	94th ('75–'76)	95th ('77–'78)	96th ('79–'80)	97th ('81–'82)	98th ('83–'84)	99th ('85–'86)
Single-committee measures						
Open	86.1	83.1	66.0	65.0	58.4	55.0
Organizing	0	1.9	0	0	1.0	0
Expansive	2.2	3.9	5.1	3.8	4.0	3.8
Closed	2.2	2.6	10.9	6.3	14.9	11.3
Restrictive	6.3	3.9	10.9	11.3	7.9	11.3
Complex	3.1	4.5	7.1	13.8	13.9	18.8
Multiple-committee measures						
Open	52.9	40.0	43.5	75.0	40.9	30.0
Organizing	17.6	13.3	13.0	0	9.1	0
Expansive	0	3.3	4.3	10.0	9.1	0
Closed	0	3.3	4.3	0	0	5.0
Restrictive	11.8	20.0	17.4	5.0	13.6	10.0
Complex	17.6	20.0	17.4	10.0	27.3	55.0
All measures[b]						
Open	81.0	75.3	62.5	64.4	54.4	49.5
Organizing	1.2	3.8	1.7	0	2.4	0
Expansive	2.0	3.8	5.0	4.8	4.8	3.0
Closed	4.4	3.8	11.0	6.7	13.6	10.9
Restrictive	7.3	6.5	11.6	10.6	8.8	10.9
Complex	4.0	7.0	8.3	13.5	16.0	25.7

SOURCES: Final *Calendars* of the House of Representatives and the Committee on Rules, and the *Congressional Record*.

a. Defined in text.

b. Includes measures that were not referred to or reported from a committee.

frequency of open rules had declined to not much more than one-half of all the special rules adopted for initial floor consideration of bills and resolutions.[23] The practices of the House had changed to such a degree that the Rules Committee no longer could be characterized as a mere "traffic cop," affecting only whether and when bills would reach the floor but not what would happen to them there. And because of the new and increasingly popular varieties of special rules, members no longer could make any confident assumptions or predictions about what procedural conditions they would encounter when the House took up bills in which they were interested.

A smattering of the rules adopted during 1975–86 were what we char-

23. Note also the significant decrease in the numbers of rules that the House considered and adopted (see table 3-1 on p. 40).

acterize as "organizing" rules—they specified the order in which certain amendments would be offered, but without restrictions that affected members' rights to offer their own amendments.[24] As we have already discussed, when two or more committees that share jurisdiction over a bill cannot reconcile their differences over it in the form of an alternative substitute, the Rules Committee may have to draft a rule arranging for members to choose between the two committees' positions, as it did in 1979 for the Alaska lands bill and in 1984 for the drug regulation bill. The resulting organizing rule lays out these arrangements without otherwise affecting noncommittee amendments. Thus these few rules are open in that they have no effect on members' opportunities to offer their own amendments.[25]

A second small set of rules, comprising no more than 5 percent of the total in any Congress, are not merely open, they are "expansive." These rules expand the bounds of an open amending process by waiving points of order that otherwise would prevent consideration of one or more non-committee amendments. If most Republicans agree on an amendment in the nature of a substitute, for example, an expansive rule may allow them to offer their alternative by waiving the germaneness rule.[26] In other instances, expansive rules advance the interests of individual members, including members of the Rules Committee itself, who have used their position to bring their own favored proposals to the floor as nongermane amendments. For instance, the 1984 rule that allowed the House to choose between competing committee amendments to a drug regulation bill also empowered the rule's Democratic floor manager, Butler Derrick of South Carolina, to offer a nongermane amendment on textile and apparel labeling.

Two other examples are illustrative. In early 1984 the House readily adopted H.Res. 350, for considering the Child Abuse Amendments of 1983, even though it waived the germaneness rule so that George Miller

24. The authors express their appreciation to Donald Wolfensberger, minority counsel to the Subcommittee on Legislative Process of the Rules Committee, for suggesting that these rules deserve to be distinguished from other open rules.

25. If certain committee amendments are considered as first-degree amendments, members can amend each of them only in the second degree, whereas they can propose amendments in two degrees to an alternative substitute that is considered as original text. So the inability of committees to reach a compromise agreement before the Rules Committee acts can limit members' opportunities to propose floor amendments. These are limitations that organizing rules recognize but do not create.

26. The Rules Committee is likely to be so generous, of course, only when the Democrats' leaders and floor managers are quite confident they have the votes to defeat the Republican substitute.

of California could offer an amendment in support of family violence prevention programs. Later, the Miller amendment, as amended, was adopted in Committee of the Whole by a vote of 367–31.[27] There was more controversy in May 1986 when, by a 257–149 margin, the House adopted H. Res. 450, for considering H.R. 1, the Housing Act of 1985. This rule made in order an alternative substitute as the text to be read for amendment and waived points of order to permit consideration of an amendment in the nature of a substitute to be offered by the bill's minority floor manager, Chalmers Wylie of Ohio. Among other things, the rule also waived the germaneness requirement to permit John Burton, a Democrat from California, to offer the same amendment to the alternative substitute and to Wylie's substitute. Under this arrangement, Burton's amendment could survive the amending process, regardless of the vote on the Wylie substitute, which ultimately lost by a margin of two to one.[28]

Adding organizing and expansive rules to the larger group of simpler and more conventional open rules does not affect the fundamental trend that table 3-2 reveals. Taken together, these three types of special rules accounted for more than five of every six rules the House adopted during 1975–76, but then steadily became less prevalent, declining to only slightly less than three out of five rules during 1983–86.

The other side of the same coin is the striking increase in the proportion of special rules limiting the opportunity of members to offer floor amendments, notwithstanding their rights under the House's standing rules. The Rules Committee has incorporated such provisions in special rules more often during the Congresses following the reforms of the 1970s, and the magnitude of this trend has been quite remarkable.

Closed Rules, Restrictive Rules

After the 1961 fight to increase the Rules Committee's size, its members were sometimes criticized for reporting "closed" rules—rules that prohibit floor amendments completely in Committee of the Whole or preclude all amendments except those recommended by the committee of jurisdiction.[29] In the course of debate on Tip O'Neill's 1970 amendment

27. *Congressional Record*, daily edition (February 2, 1984), pp. H376–422.
28. Ibid. (May 13, 1986), pp. H2646–49.
29. From the perspective of individual members, either form of rule is effectively "closed," because they cannot offer their own floor amendments. A closed rule permitting committee amendments merely leaves the committee a way of altering the position embodied in its report that is simpler and faster than convening its members once again to report a new clean bill on the same subject. And special rules that make in order only committee

to permit recorded voting in Committee of the Whole, for instance, Democrat Wayne Hays of Ohio suggested that the best way to abolish secrecy in the House would be for the Rules Committee to stop reporting closed rules on tax bills.[30] During the 94th Congress (1975–76), though, and after some of the developments discussed in chapter 2, only 4.4 percent of all special rules the House adopted were closed (table 3-2).[31] These rules also were few and far between during the 95th Congress, but then began to enjoy a modest revival: the frequency of closed rules jumped to 11 percent two years later and remained at roughly that level during two of the three following Congresses (though the numbers of rules adopted declined sharply).

Most recent closed rules have been for emergency, or at least essential, money bills, especially debt ceiling and continuing appropriations measures that are highly controversial and considered under pressure of deadlines. But there have been others as well. In particular, the Ways and Means Committee, which used to be the primary beneficiary of closed rules, has continued to seek and receive them for some of its bills, such as certain social security and trade-related legislation. In some cases, closed rules have been provoked primarily by the fear of politically irresistible floor amendments that could have jeopardized enactment of legislation that the overwhelming majority of members agreed was necessary. In others, the approach of deadlines, more than the fear of amendments, has been the major concern. The argument for a closed rule is most compelling, of course, when these two concerns coincide, as they sometimes have.[32] When Joe Moakley called up H. Res. 466 in March 1984, for instance, he asserted that a closed rule was necessary if the

---

amendments invariably preclude members from proposing amendments to these amendments. However, closed rules rarely give bills complete protection against unfriendly amendments because the minority normally retains the right to offer a motion to recommit with instructions. Thus closed rules actually constrain the majority more than the minority because the latter at least can offer one amendment via its recommittal motion.

30. *Congressional Record* (July 27, 1970), pp. 25797–98.

31. We categorize as "closed" those special rules providing for consideration of a measure "in the House" under the one-hour rule. As we noted in chapter 1, no member can propose a floor amendment under these circumstances unless a majority of members first votes not to order the previous question (or in the very unlikely event the majority floor manager does not move the previous question). In view of the fact, which all members recognize, that the House rarely rejects the previous question, rules for consideration of measures in the House are certainly intended to prevent floor amendments and almost always do so.

32. In the 99th Congress, the House adopted closed rules for considering eleven bills and resolutions, most of which fit this description, including two appropriations measures, two budget measures, and three debt ceiling measures.

House was to respond quickly to "a crisis in the social security disability program."[33] No one rose to disagree; the combination of "crisis" and "social security" evidently was compelling.

Closed rules continue to permit Democratic party and committee leaders to define the precise proposal on which the House is to vote and to prevent amendments that could undermine support for it or change its terms. But the 1973 Democratic Caucus rule by which a majority of Democrats can direct their party colleagues on Rules to make specific amendments in order opened the door to a much wider range of alternatives than the simple, dichotomous choice between open and closed rules. Much more frequently, therefore, the special rules of recent years have limited amending activity on the floor without foreclosing it altogether.[34] During the 94th Congress, 7.3 percent of the special rules adopted were not fully closed, but were "restrictive" instead; in various ways, these rules restricted what floor amendments members could propose without closing the measure to their amendments completely (see table 3-2).[35] At first, such "modified open" and "modified closed" rules were most often used for Ways and Means measures on taxes, tariffs, and social security. But in the late 1970s this pattern began to change, and by the 98th and 99th Congresses (1983–86), more than 20 percent of special rules were restrictive or closed.[36]

Restrictive provisions typically prohibit all amendments except those specifically identified or enumerated by the rule, or all amendments to certain portions of the measure or on certain subjects. However, the variations on these essential themes now are so numerous and complicated that the most conventional labels—modified open and modified closed rules—no longer do justice to their richness. We shall examine in more detail some of the ways in which special rules restrict the right of individual members, though not the reporting committee, to offer germane

33. *Congressional Record*, daily edition (March 22, 1984), pp. H1910–14.

34. For a very useful analysis, see Bruce I. Oppenheimer, "The Changing Relationship Between House Leadership and the Committee on Rules," in Frank H. Mackaman, ed., *Understanding Congressional Leadership* (Washington, D.C.: Congressional Quarterly Press, 1981), pp. 207–25.

35. In this category we include special rules providing for consideration of measures in the House as in Committee of the Whole. As soon as the House begins to consider a measure in this way, it is fully open to amendment. However, a simple majority also may vote to order the previous question on the measure and any pending amendments to it, thereby preventing consideration of all further amendments. In this sense, special rules for considering measures in the House as in Committee of the Whole are restrictive because they enable members to restrict floor amendments at will by majority vote.

36. See the discussion in chap. 5 on the changing distribution of restrictive rules among the House's reporting committees.

amendments that otherwise would be in order.[37] At this point, however, what bears emphasizing is the increase in restrictive and closed rules, taken together, from less than 12 percent of the rules adopted in the 94th Congress (1975–76) to almost 22 percent in the 99th Congress (1985–86). The import of this development becomes clear only in the context of the even more dramatic increase in "complex" special rules, characterized as such because they do not fall simply and neatly within any more limited and well-defined category. Instead, each complex rule combines characteristics of restrictive, expansive, or organizing elements. Four percent of special rules during the 94th Congress merited this characterization, but, as table 3-2 shows, their frequency increased to 13–16 percent in the 97th and 98th Congresses and to more than 25 percent in the 99th Congress. Only seven of the ninety-eight complex rules adopted during the six Congresses failed to include one or more restrictive features in addition to either expansive or organizing provisions.

To take account of the nature of most complex rules, and to put the effect of special rules on the amending process into sharper relief, we have collapsed the six distinct categories of table 3-2 into the three broader categories of table 3-3. For purposes of the latter table, "open" rules include the open, expansive, and organizing rules of the former, together with the few complex rules without restrictive provisions, while "restrictive" rules include all rules with restrictive provisions, whether or not they also include other types of provisions and so qualify as being "complex." Note the steady and marked decline in open rules during the six Congresses.[38] In the 99th Congress almost half the special rules adopted were restrictive or closed. In our view, it is the emergence of restrictive rules (including complex rules with restrictive provisions) that is the most interesting and significant development.[39]

The appeal of special rules with restrictive provisions is greatest to majority floor leaders and bill managers when the outcome of votes on

37. It is important to bear in mind that even the most severe restrictions on floor amendments rarely apply to committee amendments—those amendments approved by vote of the reporting committee. Thus the committee of jurisdiction typically retains the flexibility to offer amendments to make necessary technical corrections or, more important, to respond to changes in political or policy circumstances.

38. Donald Wolfensberger also has compiled data that are consistent with this conclusion. See the statement by Representative Lott on H. Res. 265, the rule for the Agricultural Credit Act of 1987, in *Congressional Record*, daily edition (September 21, 1987), p. H7639. The differences between his data and those presented here merely demonstrate that categorizing special rules involves judgments on which informed observers will differ.

39. See Barbara Sinclair, *Majority Leadership in the U.S. House* (Johns Hopkins University Press, 1983), pp. 77–85.

TABLE 3-3. Frequency of Open, Restrictive, and Closed Rules, for All
Measures and Key Vote Measures, 94th–99th Congresses (1975 86)[a]
Percent

Type of rule	Congress					
	94th ('75–'76)	95th ('77–'78)	96th ('79–'80)	97th ('81–'82)	98th ('83–'84)	99th ('85–'86)
All measures						
Open	84.3	83.9	68.9	71.2	64.0	55.4
Restrictive	11.3	12.4	20.0	22.1	22.4	33.7
Closed	4.4	3.8	11.1	6.7	13.6	10.9
N	248	186	180	104	125	101
Key vote measures[b]						
Open	63.6	70.6	52.0	23.5	31.8	13.6
Restrictive	31.8	23.5	40.0	64.7	63.6	72.7
Closed	4.5	5.9	8.0	11.8	4.5	13.6
N	22	17	25	17	22	22

SOURCES: Final *Calendars* of the House of Representatives and the Committee on Rules, and the *Congressional Record.*
a. See the text for an explanation of the criteria for combining the categories of table 3-2 into those of this table.
b. Measures in connection with which there was at least one "key vote," as identified by *Congressional Quarterly.*

critical amendments is most uncertain and when the policy and political
consequences of losing are greatest. The political logic favoring restrictive
rules flows readily from some of the developments chronicled in chapter
2. Much of the basis for deference to committees on the floor has been
undermined, thanks in part to subcommittee decentralization and multiple referrals. Members of the House, including junior and Republican
members and members not on the reporting committee, have become
more likely to offer floor amendments, and, because of the availability of
recorded teller votes, more likely to win. As a result, it has become harder
for majority bill managers, and party leaders attempting to assist them, to
approach floor debates with confidence that they can anticipate amendments and muster the votes to defeat them. Requiring that the amendments be printed in advance in the *Record* addresses one difficulty, but
not the other. The most effective response, therefore, is for the Rules
Committee to propose, and for the House to adopt, special rules that
restrict amending activity, thereby minimizing uncertainty about what
will be offered and allowing bill managers to concentrate their defensive
efforts.[40]

40. At the same time, restrictive rules must put a strain on the Democratic leadership's
formal whip system and informal intelligence networks. When members expect a restrictive
rule, as they now must do more and more often, they have to expose their amendments to
their colleagues when they testify before the Rules Committee. But the committee then
must rely on Democratic party and committee leaders, as well as its own judgment, to

Restrictive rules should be particularly popular for considering difficult bills, and this is what emerges clearly from a comparison of the two parts of table 3-3. For the most major, controversial measures—or at least those involving one of the "key" votes identified each year by *Congressional Quarterly*—the trend toward rules restricting floor amendments has been even more pronounced and consistent. Of the "key vote" bills for which the House adopted special rules in the 94th and 95th Congresses (1975–78), about one-third received rules that were restrictive or closed; during the 98th and 99th Congresses (1983–86), by contrast, about three-quarters of such bills were considered under restrictive or closed rules. The House adopted open rules for considering less than 14 percent of the "key vote" measures during the 99th Congress (1985–86). The pattern of the last three Congresses must now lead members to expect that the Rules Committee will propose restrictive rules for bills such as these, and, what is just as important, that a majority of members will be prepared to vote for them.

The Uses of Restrictive Rules

The movement toward special rules restricting floor amendments has been a development of extraordinary significance for the House. Consider the 1987 negotiations among House and Senate leaders of both parties with President Reagan's representatives to agree on a deficit reduction package consisting of a balanced combination of domestic and defense spending reductions and revenue increases. As the Democratic and Republican House leaders engaged in these negotiations, they undoubtedly assumed that, with the cooperation of the Rules Committee, they would have the option of bringing the two resulting measures to the House floor under special rules restricting floor amendments. Such rules obviously were necessary to preclude politically appealing amendments that would have destroyed the fragile agreement. Only with restrictive rules could they hope to include in the bills any changes in programs that enjoyed intense and widespread constituent support, such as social security and other entitlement programs. In fact, the possibility of including a delay

---

gauge which amendments would pose real dangers on the floor. (If an unfriendly amendment is certain to lose, it may be politically advantageous to allow it to be offered.) The problem is that it can be very difficult, if not impossible, to get an accurate reading of members' sentiments on a prospective floor amendment in time for the Rules Committee's markup. Even if members have formed a clear opinion of the amendment so far in advance, which they often have not, they may not wish to express it at this stage, even to their party colleagues.

or reduction in social security cost of living adjustments was stalled when Chairman Pepper of the Rules Committee announced that "he would insist on a separate vote on that provision on the House floor."[41]

Veterans of presidential-congressional relations have lamented the passing of the days in which the president could negotiate with one or more committee chairmen with full confidence that the chairmen then could return to Capitol Hill and "deliver." These negotiations made political sense because effective chairmen usually could prevail on the House floor when it was most important for them to do so. After the process of subcommittee decentralization began in the 1970s, there were complaints that such negotiations were hampered by the need to consult and coordinate with the large number of members who laid claim to some part of policy turf as subcommittee chairmen or ranking minority members. There also were doubts that even party leaders could commit their colleagues on difficult policy choices. The emergence of restrictive rules in the 1980s appears to have changed this dynamic once again. Such "domestic summit" negotiations now are predicated on assumptions that the House will accept restrictive provisions for considering the resulting package—even if, in the process, members deny themselves the chance to consider amendments which, if offered, they would support.

Since the inception of multiple referrals, as this line of argument suggests, multiple-committee bills have been more likely than others to receive restrictive rules or complex rules with restrictive provisions. As table 3-4 shows, this difference has persisted while the popularity of such rules for both kinds of measures has increased.[42] The chances of the

41. Tom Kenworthy, "Hope Dims for Friday Budget Accord," *Washington Post*, November 17, 1987, p. A6. On the 1987 continuing resolution, see H. Res. 321, the restrictive rule for considering H. J. Res. 395. *Congressional Record*, daily edition (December 3, 1987), pp. H10900–11. And on the reconciliation bill for that year, see H. Res. 296, which the House rejected, and H. Res. 298, which the House adopted, both restrictive rules for considering H.R. 3545. *Congressional Record*, daily edition (October 29, 1987), pp. H9130–41, H9158–66.

42. Davidson and Oleszek, "From Monopoly to Interaction," pp. 18, 49, came to a different conclusion based on their data for the 98th Congress. They adopted somewhat different categories for classifying rules than those employed here, but that does not seem sufficient to account fully for the contrasting conclusions. There are at least three other probable explanations for the difference between their findings and ours. First, they examined rules granted for singly and multiply referred measures, while this analysis considers rules granted and adopted (without substantive amendment) for single- and multiple-committee measures, as defined earlier in the text. Second, we have excluded certain kinds of rules from this analysis (see note 22). And third, they evidently used the characterizations (such as "modified open rule," "modified closed rule") that accompany the summaries of special rules made by Rules Committee staff and reported in the committee's *Legislative Calendars*, while the data presented here are based instead on the authors' assessment of the

TABLE 3-4. Frequency of Special Rules for Single- and Multiple-Committee Measures, 94th–99th Congresses (1975–86)

Percent

	Congress					
Type of measure and rule	94th ('75–'76)	95th ('77–'78)	96th ('79–'80)	97th ('81–'82)	98th ('83–'84)	99th ('85–'86)
Single-committee measures						
Open	88.3	90.3	71.0	71.3	66.3	61.3
Restrictive	9.4	7.1	18.1	22.5	18.8	27.5
Closed	2.2	2.6	11.0	6.3	14.9	11.3
N	223	154	155	80	101	80
Multiple-committee measures						
Open	70.6	56.7	60.9	85.0	59.1	35.0
Restrictive	29.4	40.0	34.8	15.0	40.9	60.0
Closed	0	3.3	4.3	0	0	5.0
N	17	30	23	20	22	20

SOURCES: Final *Calendars* of the House of Representatives and the Committee on Rules, and the *Congressional Record*.

House adopting a restrictive rule in 1975 or 1976 were 9.4 percent for a single-committee bill and 29.4 percent for a multiple-committee bill; in 1985 and 1986, by contrast, 27.5 percent of single-committee measures received restrictive rules, as did fully 60 percent of multiple-committee bills. Taking closed rules into account as well, only 35 percent of multiple-committee bills considered in 1985–86 were fully open to amendment under the terms of special rules.

Even when there is no omnibus legislative package at stake, as in the case of reconciliation bills, there are several reasons why committee and subcommittee chairmen often choose to request that the Rules Committee grant restrictive rules for their multiple-committee bills. We have noted that such bills tend, on average, to be broader and more controversial than single-committee measures and so would be more likely under any circumstances to attract numerous floor amendments, some of them politically divisive and dangerous. If the two (or more) committees take incompatible positions, an open conflict between them on the floor may stimulate other members to propose their own amendments unless prevented from doing so by a restrictive rule. On the other hand, if the committee leaders agree in advance on a compromise for the Rules Com-

summaries and, when necessary, an examination of the resolutions themselves. The differences we discuss in the text are consistent with the impressions and comments of several Rules Committee members and staff.

mittee to make in order as an alternative substitute, a restriction on floor amendments still may be necessary to protect the delicate intercommittee agreement from collapsing. During each of the six Congresses, in fact, rules providing for alternative substitutes were more likely than others to be either restrictive or closed. According to Rules Committee members, on several occasions they even offered protective rules to committee or subcommittee chairmen as an incentive to negotiate a compromise between their positions.

The resulting arrangement suits all the Democratic parties to it. The reporting committees are at least partially insulated from attack on the floor; the floor leaders avoid amendments that would divide their forces; and the Rules Committee satisfies both, while also benefiting from the well-understood expectation that Democrats should support their party leaders, including the Rules Committee, on "procedural" votes. The Republicans on Rules sometimes support these kinds of arrangements because they also avoid tortuous, time-consuming floor fights, an especially attractive advantage at the approach of deadlines such as the end of the fiscal year. More often, however, Republicans object to having been excluded from development of the alternative substitute and to being prevented from offering all the floor amendments they would like.

Variety in Restrictive Rules

Each open rule is very much like every other, as is each closed rule. But there is room for considerable variety in the ways in which and the extent to which restrictive rules affect the amending process. And just as the frequency of restrictive rules has changed over the six Congresses we are examining here, so too have there been changes in the nature of their restrictive provisions, as table 3-5 documents. The restrictive provisions of special rules adopted by the House during these Congresses are divisible into four categories.

In the 94th Congress (1975–76), none of these categories was dominant. First, 14 percent of these rules permitted amendments only to certain provisions of measures or committee amendments or only on certain subjects the measures addressed. H. Res. 1093, for example, which the House adopted on March 23, 1976, brought H.R. 10799 before the House for consideration. The bill proposed to amend the Economic Opportunity Act of 1964 regarding the authority of the Legal Services Corporation. To preclude amendments affecting other aspects of the corporation's activities, the rule provided in part that:

TABLE 3-5. Types of Restrictive Provisions in Special Rules, 94th–99th Congresses (1975–86)[a]

Percent

Type of restrictive provision	Congress					
	94th ('75–'76)	95th ('77–'78)	96th ('79–'80)	97th ('81–'82)	98th ('83–'84)	99th ('85–'86)
Restricting amendments to those that would amend certain provisions or committee amendments or on certain subjects	14.3	9.5	17.2	4.2	0	0
Restricting amendments to those printed in the *Congressional Record*	23.8	28.6	6.9	12.5	3.7	13.3
Prohibiting amendments (or all but 1–2 amendments) to certain provisions or committee amendments or on certain subjects	28.6	28.6	6.9	8.3	11.1	10.0
Restricting amendments to those listed in the special rule or accompanying Rules Committee report	33.3	28.6	55.2	75.0	77.8	66.7
Combination of the above	0	4.8	13.8	0	7.4	10.0
N	21	21	29	24	27	30

a. This table excludes special rules for considering measures in the House as in Committee of the Whole, and therefore subject to the previous question, as well as six rules with other types of provisions. These data, like the other data on special rules presented here, are derived primarily from the summaries of special rules contained in the final *Calendars* of the House Rules Committee. These summaries were assumed to be accurate and complete unless ambiguous or incomplete on their face, in which case the actual texts of, and debates on, the special rules were examined in the *Congressional Record*. The special rules on which data are presented here are those characterized in table 3–2 as restrictive or complex rules, though the totals in this table do not equal the sums of restrictive and complex rules for the same Congresses in table 3–2, because of the few complex rules without pertinent restrictive provisions. This table addresses only those restrictions affecting first-degree amendments offered from the floor by individual members; it ignores any provisions of special rules affecting consideration of committee amendments. The restrictions in the first and third categories may apply to amendments to a measure, to part or parts of a measure, or to one or more committee amendments. A few special rules are credited here with having more than one principal characteristic. This table constitutes a necessarily imperfect attempt to fit considerable complexity and variability into a limited number of clearly distinguishable categories.

No amendments shall be in order to the bill in the House or in the Committee of the Whole amending any provisions of the Economic Opportunity Act of 1964, as amended, except amendments to section 1006(a)(3) of said Act which relate solely to the method of delivery of those support activities provided under that subsection and amendments germane to section 1010(d), as proposed to be added to said Act by section 2 of the bill.[43]

Speaking for the Republicans on Rules, Trent Lott argued that "it has been the policy of this body to avoid the use of closed rules with the exception of legislation reported from the Ways and Means Committee and certain other instances."[44] But his opposition was perfunctory; the House agreed to the rule by a vote of 343–44.

Second, slightly less than one-fourth of these special rules restricted amendments to those that had been printed in advance in the *Congressional Record,* for reasons discussed above. The Rules Committee turned to this device in 1975, for instance, after the Judiciary Committee reported H.R. 6799, a particularly complicated measure amending the federal rules of criminal procedure. H. Res. 513 did not prevent consideration of germane amendments, but instead gave Judiciary Committee members and staff an opportunity to examine them before the amending process began:

No amendment shall be in order to the bill except amendments offered by direction of the Committee on the Judiciary or germane amendments printed in the Congressional Record at least two calendar days prior to the start of consideration of said bill for amendment, but said amendments shall not be subject to amendment except those offered by direction of the Committee on the Judiciary.[45]

The Republican manager of the rule, Delbert Latta, supported it, explaining that "this bill will come up for general debate only tomorrow, and then it will lay over for 6 days to give the membership an opportunity to examine the legislation and to have proposed amendments printed in the Record."[46] As we have illustrated, not all rules with such advance notice requirements have been quite so accommodating.

Third, a somewhat larger share of the restrictive rules adopted during

43. *Congressional Record* (March 23, 1976), p. 7686.
44. Ibid.
45. Ibid. (June 5, 1975), p. 17164.
46. Ibid.

the 94th Congress prohibited all (or almost all) amendments to certain provisions or committee amendments or amendments on certain subjects, especially to protect legislation from the Ways and Means Committee. The 1975 bill to provide emergency financial assistance to New York City, for example, fell within the jurisdiction of both the Banking and the Ways and Means committees. Under H. Res. 865, which the House adopted on December 2, 1975, title I from the Banking Committee was fully open to amendment, but not title II:

> No amendment to title II of said bill shall be in order except amendments recommended by the Committee on Ways and Means, and said amendments shall not be subject to amendment.[47]

It was almost as if there were two rules governing action on the same bill—an open rule for the Banking Committee legislation, and a closed rule to give Ways and Means legislation the insulation from amendments it had so often enjoyed.

And finally, fully one-third of the restrictive rules limited amendments to those specifically printed, listed, or otherwise designated in the special rule itself. Consider the rule on the Tax Reform Act of 1975. The day after debating the New York City rule discussed above, the House took up H. Res. 878, which precluded all amendments to the tax bill except Ways and Means Committee amendments and seven others—five to be offered by Abner Mikva, Democrat of Illinois, and one by each of two other Democrats, James Jones of Oklahoma and Neal Smith of Iowa. Moreover, none of these amendments was amendable except by the committee. On behalf of the Rules Committee, Bolling said that the rule reflected the request made by the chairman of Ways and Means, except for the addition of the Smith amendment. Bolling also observed wryly that there "seems to be a difference between the parties on this matter." Mikva also called attention to the fact that Ways and Means had not requested a closed rule, as it almost certainly would have done even five years earlier. In fact, Mikva argued, "I do not remember any tax bill in which the House had anywhere near as much input in the bill as they will have if this rule is adopted."[48]

But the Republicans were far from convinced. John Anderson de-

47. Ibid. (December 2, 1975), p. 38135. The effect of the rule was more or less nullified when the Committee of the Whole ultimately adopted an amendment in the nature of a substitute for all titles of the bill.
48. Ibid. (December 3, 1975), pp. 38269, 38273.

scribed what had happened in the Rules Committee's hearing and markup:

> Mr. Speaker, the Rules Committee sat for three days on this rule and heard from some 24 witnesses. Many of those witnesses pleaded with the Rules Committee to make additional amendments in order. Attempts were made by a minority of the majority party, and by all of the Republican members, to further open this bill to those amendments. . . . On the Republican side, motions were offered to provide for a completely open rule, a rule which would permit the offering of amendments considered and voted on by the Ways and Means Committee, and a rule which would permit striking out sections of the bill. All of these alternative rules were turned back—many along party-line votes.[49]

Instead, the rule allowed three Democrats to monopolize the amending process, and Ways and Means members (Mikva and Jones) to offer six of the seven amendments that individual members were allowed to offer. According to Joe Waggonner, a conservative Democratic member of the tax committee, "a limited number of people are able to get consideration for measures which they lost over and over again in the committee."[50] In other words, the rule allowed the two Ways and Means Democrats to appeal their losses during markup by offering floor amendments. Such appeals were precisely what the Democratic Caucus had intended when it gave itself the authority to instruct the Democrats on Rules to make certain amendments in order, but in this case, no such instructions had been necessary. In reaction, Anderson urged the House to vote against ordering the previous question, but not so that he could propose an open rule as a substitute. His amendment to the rule would have allowed two Republican amendments in addition to the seven for which it already provided. Even so, the House ordered the previous question, 219–197, and then agreed to the resolution by voice vote. The Rules Committee evidently had calculated correctly that the Republicans would not succeed in devising an alternative that would attract enough disgruntled Democrats to form a winning coalition.

The Democratic Caucus did intervene in August of the following year. When Claude Pepper called up H. Res. 1496, for considering the Estate and Gift Tax Reform Act of 1976, also reported by Ways and Means, he

49. Ibid., p. 38269.
50. Ibid., p. 38271.

explained why the rule permitted two amendments by Mikva but no others:

> These two amendments, if I am informed correctly, were in the original bill offered by the chairman of the Ways and Means Committee. After a rather close vote, as I understand it, the amendments finally . . . were eliminated by a majority of the Ways and Means Committee. But the Democratic Caucus directed the Democratic members of the Rules Committee to support these two amendments because I suppose a majority of the Democratic Caucus thought the amendments had merit or at least they were of such merit and character as to deserve consideration by this House.[51]

Anderson and his fellow Republicans responded by invoking the image of "King Caucus" dictating to members of both parties. And this time his alternative was a rule that simply imposed an advance notice requirement unaccompanied by any other restrictions on amendments—a far cry from the closed rule Ways and Means originally had requested and was accustomed to receiving. With a substitute that was better designed to appeal to disaffected Democrats, Anderson prevailed when the roll call came on ordering the previous question, because he had the support of influential Ways and Means Democrats J. J. Pickle and Charles Vanik, among others. In this case, the Democrats on Rules had miscalculated, or perhaps they had been precluded from exercising their own judgment by the directive they had received from the caucus.

Over the succeeding Congresses, the first three types of restrictive rules have become less common, decreasing in frequency in favor of special rules illustrated by these last two examples—rules that identify the amendments that members may propose and exclude all others. Two out of every three restrictive rules the House adopted during 1985–86 took this basic form, barring all amendments except the chosen few.

This pattern of change probably represents an instance of institutional learning. As Rules Committee members and others started thinking in terms of alternatives to the simple choice between open or closed rules, the most obvious approach was to apply each of these familiar forms to different parts of the same measure—prohibiting amendments altogether to some sections (or titles) of a bill, while leaving its other parts fully open to amendment. And such hybrid rules were an equally natural way of coping with one product of multiple referrals—bills that fell partially, but

---

51. Ibid. (August 30, 1976), p. 28305.

TABLE 3-6. Frequency of Special Rules Making Only Certain Amendments in Order, by Number of Amendments, 94th–99th Congresses (1975–86)

Percent

	Congress					
Number of amendments in order	94th ('75–'76)	95th ('77–'78)	96th ('79–'80)	97th ('81–'82)	98th ('83–'84)	99th ('85–'86)
1–2	28.6	33.3	60.0	61.1	61.9	50.0
3–6	42.8	16.7	33.3	22.2	19.0	30.0
7–12	14.3	50.0	6.7	5.5	14.3	5.0
13 or more	14.3	0	0	11.1	4.8	15.0
Total	100.0	100.0	100.0	99.9	100.0	100.0
N	7	6	15	18	21	20

SOURCES: Final *Calendars* of the Committee on Rules and various issues of the *Congressional Record*.

not wholly, within the jurisdiction of the Ways and Means Committee. Under the precedents governing multiple referrals, if a bill proposes to impose or raise a tax and then to establish a program or designate a purpose for which the resulting revenues are to be used, the former provisions are a Ways and Means responsibility. The Rules Committee could respond to multiply referred bills with revenue provisions by sending them to the House floor under special rules that were closed with respect to the Ways and Means sections or title, but open with respect to the programmatic provisions reported by the other committee (or committees). The rule for the 1975 bill to aid New York City exemplified this approach.

Then, as the House became more familiar with the concept and effect of restrictive rules and demonstrated a willingness to adopt them under appropriate circumstances, and as the Rules Committee and the Democratic leadership recognized their advantages, they started exploring other ways in which special rules could restrict floor amendments. The four principal forms of restrictions discussed above developed; then one of them gradually emerged as preferable far more often than the others because, we suspect, it offered the most effective management strategy for handling uncertainty on the floor.

When a special rule identifies all possible floor amendments, the Democratic bill manager and his committee allies can concentrate on evaluating them, calculating the most effective responses, and working with the Democratic party leadership—including its elaborate whip system—to construct winning coalitions on the anticipated floor votes. So the burden on bill managers and party leaders is reduced substantially, especially when the rule makes few amendments in order. As table 3-6 shows, most restrictive rules of this kind adopted during the 96th–99th Congresses (1979–86) provided for only one or two floor amendments in addition to committee amendments, and 80 to 90 percent of these rules permitted consideration of no more than half a dozen amendments.

Partisan Use of Restrictive Rules

The greater restrictiveness of special rules in this decade no doubt reflects the much more defensive posture into which House Democratic leaders were thrust after the 1980 election, when Republicans assumed control of the Senate as well as the White House. When the 97th Congress convened in 1981, the Speaker and the Rules Committee confronted a larger and energized Republican minority, as well as many Democrats who were very sensitive to President Reagan's popularity in their districts. It soon became clear that unfriendly floor amendments were more likely to win than at any time in the recent past; and, given Republican control of the Senate and the White House, these losses could not be recouped in conference negotiations or by presidential vetoes. So during the first years of the Reagan administration restrictive rules became much more than a useful way of compensating for the uncertainty of floor outcomes. They also became a partisan response to the clear and present danger that the Committee of the Whole might well adopt major unwelcome amendments if members had opportunities to offer them.[52]

Thus, as a convergence of political and institutional developments increased the likelihood of Democratic party and committee defeats on the floor, majority party leaders turned to the House's standing rules as well as the Rules Committee's special rules to keep unfriendly proposals from reaching the floor at all. It became important to keep bills and resolutions on these subjects in the filing cabinets of the House's committees—the Judiciary Committee, for example, with jurisdiction over highly charged issues such as abortion, busing, and school prayer.[53] The Democratic leaders also sought to prevent members from circumventing the committee system and bringing their proposals directly to the floor as amend-

52. See, for example, Steven S. Smith, "The Budget Battles of 1981: The Role of the Majority Party Leadership," in Allan P. Sindler, ed., *American Politics and Public Policy: Seven Case Studies* (Washington, D.C.: Congressional Quarterly Press, 1982), pp. 43–78; and Sinclair's outstanding study, *Majority Leadership in the U.S. House.*

53. In this regard, it was fortunate for Democratic leaders that changes in caucus rules, and the recollection that the caucus had defeated committee chairmen for reelection after the 1974 election, had given chairmen more reason to be responsive to the prevailing views of their fellow Democrats by keeping such measures in committee.

ments, especially as limitation amendments to general appropriations bills. To this end, as we noted in chapter 2, the House amended Rule XXI at the beginning of the 98th Congress (1983) to allow a majority of members to vote against considering any such amendment.[54]

So the growth of restrictive provisions in special rules must be seen in this larger context of Democratic efforts during the early 1980s to avoid floor votes that would have been politically embarrassing and on which their reduced and more fragile majority might not have held together. But it would be a mistake to conclude that the trend toward restrictive rules arose exclusively from partisan motivations. While the increase in floor amendments was a danger to the majority leadership, it was a nuisance for all members. Controversial bills remained on the floor for hour after hour, floor sessions extended into the evening, the floor schedule became less predictable, and key policy choices could be lost in the shuffle of amendment after amendment. In many cases, therefore, restrictive rules won bipartisan support from Rules Committee members on the ground that they focused the attention of members on the limited number of key decisions that were at issue.

In still other instances, the committee has gone to such lengths to ensure that a restrictive rule accommodated members' preferences and intentions that it strains the meaning of the word to characterize the rule as "restrictive." A notable case in point was the special rule the House adopted in June 1984 to consider the Simpson-Mazzoli immigration reform bill. This rule prohibited all amendments—except for the sixty-nine amendments printed in the accompanying Rules Committee report. The Republican floor manager of the rule, Minority Whip Trent Lott, applauded the rule:

> It was made clear at the outset that those wishing to have amendments made in order should officially appear before us during our hearings and make available copies of their amendments. I think we have managed to accommodate nearly all of those Members who met those requirements and had germane amendments to offer. I think our initial count after the hearings showed some 87 amendments had been submitted; another 19 were submitted after the deadline. But, of those 87 we have made in order 69 in this rule. So, the Rules Committee did make every effort to be as fair as possible while at the same time structuring this complicated process in

54. Another proposed rules change, which the caucus failed to recommend, would have addressed the same general problem by requiring a two-thirds vote to discharge House committees from further consideration of proposed constitutional amendments.

a way to insure that we could reach a conclusion in the amendment process in a reasonable time. . . . [55]

This extremely controversial bill created serious and emotion-laden divisions within the Democratic majority, and it is in precisely such cases that the Rules Committee adopts the most neutral possible posture. The committee did not want to pick and choose among the amendments that members wished to offer; members' interests were too intense, and there was no true Democratic party position, except the need to pass a bill, to protect against amendments. The committee simply could have proposed an open rule instead, as it surely would have done under comparable circumstances in decades past. But that is precisely how the House had debated an incarnation of the same bill at the end of the 97th Congress (1982), only to see it fall victim to an effective threat of a filibuster-by-amendment by opponents who submitted an imposing string of amendments for printing in the *Record*, assuring themselves of ten minutes of debate and the possibility of a recorded vote on each of them.[56]

At various times, therefore, restrictive rules have served the interests of the committees reporting legislation by making prospective floor developments more predictable and manageable, the interests of the majority party and its leaders by preventing unwelcome amendments from reaching the floor, and the interests of the House as an institution by keeping the amending process within constructive bounds.[57] One way of exploring the relative importance of these effects is to examine the provisions of the restrictive rules that precluded consideration of all but specifically designated noncommittee amendments in order to determine how often these rules gave the Democratic party or the reporting committee, or both, monopoly control over the floor amendments in order.

We find that the proportions of these restrictive rules providing for

---

55. *Congressional Record*, daily edition (June 11, 1984), p. H5530.

56. In the event of such dilatory tactics, the Rules Committee can report a second rule governing further consideration of the bill or resolution. In 1987 the committee and the House agreed on three rules for considering the defense authorization bill, not in response to deliberate delay, but as a planned and well-calibrated way of coping with the burgeoning number of amendments that members wanted to offer. In all, these rules permitted consideration of more than one hundred amendments, several times more than members had proposed to comparable bills under open rules just a few years earlier.

57. "In 1983, a nuclear-freeze bill generated dozens of amendments and 40 hours of debate over a two-month period, and created an embarrassing atmosphere of chaos for the Democratic majority. After that, House leaders and the Rules Committee kept the terms of debate and amendment under tight control. Rarely did discussion of even the most controversial bill take more than a couple of days. Few sessions lasted past 7 P.M." *Congressional Quarterly Almanac*, vol. 42 (1986), p. 34.

majority party or committee monopoly of floor amendments have been fairly high throughout the period. Of such restrictive rules adopted during the 94th-96th Congresses (1975–80), 44 percent permitted only Democratic amendments and 42 percent permitted only amendments sponsored by members from the reporting committee (or committees). There was essentially no change during the next six years; the corresponding figures were 42 percent and 38 percent, respectively, in the 97th–99th Congresses (1981–86).[58] While committee members are more likely than others to have amendments to their bills, their disproportionate interest hardly can account for the frequency of committee monopolies. And, as a general rule, Republicans should have more incentive than Democrats to offer floor amendments, as minority party members attempt to reverse defeats in committee. So it is true that a majority of restrictive rules have not totally foreclosed amendments by minority and noncommittee members.[59] But it is equally true, and undoubtedly more important, that the Rules Committee often has written special rules with a strong bias toward party and committee interests.

Effect on Amending Activity

Given these patterns and trends, to what extent has the shift toward restrictive rules actually suppressed floor amending activity? A look back at tables 2-1 and 2-3 indicates that amending activity peaked about the time of the 95th Congress (1977–78) and then declined in the 1980s, a pattern

58. It bears emphasizing that the remaining restrictive rules were not necessarily as generous to Republicans as to Democrats and to noncommittee members as to committee members. We are only distinguishing here between restrictive rules that barred all Republican or noncommittee members' amendments and those that did not.

59. It should be noted that closed rules permitting only committee amendments, as well as restrictive rules providing for Democratic monopoly control over floor amendments in Committee of the Whole, usually do not foreclose consideration in the House of a Republican amendment as part of a motion to recommit with instructions. Clause 4(b) of Rule XI specifically prohibits the Rules Committee from reporting "any rule or order which would prevent the motion to recommit from being made as provided in clause 4 of Rule XVI" (*House Rules and Manual*, pp. 459–62). Of motions to recommit with instructions, Republican Whip Trent Lott contended that "just as the power to preside is a prerogative of the Speaker, the right to offer recommittal instructions is a sacred prerogative of the minority." *Congressional Record*, daily edition (May 24, 1988), p. H3578. Yet Lott reported that twelve special rules during the 99th Congress had prohibited recommittal motions from containing any instructions or specific kinds of instructions or had achieved the same end indirectly by prohibiting consideration of certain amendments in Committee of the Whole or in the House. This compared with only one such rule throughout the 95th–98th Congresses. (Data compiled by Donald Wolfensberger.)

TABLE 3-7. Mean Number of Floor Amendments Offered and Adopted under Special Rules, by Type of Rule, 94th–99th Congresses (1975–86)

	Congress					
Type of rule	94th ('75–'76)	95th ('77–'78)	96th ('79–'80)	97th ('81–'82)	98th ('83–'84)	99th ('85–'86)
Amendments offered per measure						
Open	4.5	7.3	6.4	6.4	7.7	5.4
Restrictive	5.1	8.0	3.4	6.7	7.5	16.6
Closed	0	0	0	0	0	0
Amendments adopted per measure						
Open	2.5	4.7	4.6	4.3	5.3	4.3
Restrictive	2.7	4.5	2.4	3.6	5.6	12.7
Closed	0	0	0	0	0	0

that is generally consistent with the growth of restrictive rules.[60] Yet the distribution of amending activity among the basic types of rules, depicted in table 3-7, shows relatively little difference, except during the 96th Congress (1979–80), between the mean number of amendments per measure that were offered or adopted under restrictive rules and those offered or adopted under open rules. During the 94th, 95th, and 97th Congresses, in fact, there was slightly more amending activity, on average, under restrictive rules. The one striking difference emerged during the 99th Congress (1985–86), when three times as many amendments per measure were offered and adopted under restrictive rules than under open rules.

Part of the explanation lies in the fact that not all restrictive rules are very restrictive. For instance, a rule imposing an advance notice requirement on amendments imposes a far less severe restriction than one permitting only certain designated amendments to be offered. And as the rule for the Simpson-Mazzoli immigration bill illustrated, even restrictive rules that allow members to offer only certain designated amendments

60. Undoubtedly there have been other developments, such as the popularity of suspension motions, that have contributed to the declining number of floor amendments in recent Congresses. Another possible cause of the decline may lie in the degree to which the congressional agenda has been truncated by the politics of budget deficits. The number of new policy initiatives, whether embodied in separate bills or floor amendments, has fallen, a trend that has been reflected in most measures of work load in the House during the 1980s. And budget politics also has contributed to another development that we noted earlier: omnibus bills, usually massive continuing appropriations and reconciliation measures, which have restructured the floor agenda in a way that has reduced the number of targets for floor amendments. The intimidating size and complexity of these bills might well have had a discouraging effect on members' amending activity even if there had been no such thing as restrictive rules.

TABLE 3-8. Frequency of Floor Amendments Proposed under Special
Rules, by Type of Rule, 94th–99th Congresses (1975–86)
Percent

| Type of rule | Congress | | | | | |
	94th ('75–'76)	95th ('77–'78)	96th ('79–'80)	97th ('81–'82)	98th ('83–'84)	99th ('85–'86)
Open	86.9	86.1	86.9	75.4	74.6	35.0[a]
Restrictive	13.1	13.9	13.1	24.6	25.4	65.0[a]
Closed	0	0	0	0	0	0
N	1,088	1,316	921	631	822	868

a. When measures subject to fifty or more amendments are excluded, the percentage of amendments proposed under open rules is 65.2 and under restrictive rules is 34.8. Making the same adjustment has little effect on the results for prior Congresses.

can still be quite generous in the numbers of amendments that are in order. If measures to which members offered fifty or more amendments are set aside, the differences in 99th Congress amending activity virtually disappear. The mean number of amendments offered under restrictive rules drops to 5.4 and the mean number adopted under restrictive rules drops to 3.7.[61]

These data serve to illustrate that some restrictive rules have not been intended to constrain members so much as to accommodate their wishes while organizing and defining the outer limits of what still can be an extended amending process. In these cases, the intent of special rules is to minimize uncertainty about process, not about policy—to control in advance what alternatives will be presented, not what the final shape of legislation will be. However many amendments members offer, at least they do not come as surprises under restrictive rules. Table 3-8 documents the Rules Committee's success in protecting against unexpected floor amendments. In the 94th–96th Congresses (1975–80), more than 80 percent of amendments were offered under open rules. A decline then began in the 97th Congress, and by the 99th Congress much of the uncertainty about what floor amendments would be offered, and by whom, had been eliminated.

As we have discussed, the Rules Committee has proposed some restrictive rules in order to preclude one or more particularly unwelcome amendments. More often, though, it brings such rules to the floor precisely because it anticipates that members otherwise would offer a substantial (or excessive) number of amendments. Members usually have

61. When the same adjustment is made for the earlier Congresses, the differences are very small. The data are not shown in the table.

proposed at least as many amendments under restrictive rules as under open rules in part because of the nature of the bills at issue. To put it more directly, major bills attract amendments and therefore receive restrictive rules. By limiting floor amendments, these rules suppress some amendments that members otherwise would propose. But the Rules Committee must be careful. If it makes the restrictions too severe, it faces defeat.

Innovation and Creativity

As restrictive rules became more common and even conventional, members naturally began to consider how essentially the same instrument could be adapted and refined into a more flexible and still more useful way of limiting and defining the policy choices to be made during the amending process. Moreover, it undoubtedly was no coincidence that the Rules Committee's Democratic leader during this period was Richard Bolling, one of the House's acknowledged experts in its legislative procedures. Bolling combined this knowledge with a majority party leadership perspective to develop an innovative repertoire of devices that has continued to evolve and expand since his retirement in 1982. From this still developing repertoire, the Rules Committee now can choose the components of special rules—selecting, refining, and assembling them into the combination most appropriate for each measure.

One indication of this development is the increasing number of complex rules, which include expansive, organizing, or other features in addition to one or more restrictive provisions. As we already have pointed out, complex rules were almost unknown during the 94th Congress, but constituted more than one-quarter of all the special rules the House adopted during the 99th Congress. Among these rules are examples of two recent innovations that the Rules Committee has developed for arranging or controlling the House's deliberations when circumstances warrant.

"King-of-the-Mountain" Rules

The first of these innovations has become known as the "king-of-the-mountain" or "king-of-the-hill" rule. It typically provides for votes on a series of alternative versions of a measure; but if a majority votes for more than one of the alternatives, only the last of them wins. In the process, this kind of rule sets aside a fundamental principle of the normal amending process: that an amendment may not propose to amend only a portion of a bill (or amendment) that already has been amended. This prohibition against reamending means that once the House agrees to an amendment in the nature of a substitute, all portions of the measure have been amended and so no further amendments to it are in order. When one complete substitute is proposed, a second can be offered as an alternative to it; but if a majority votes for either of these two versions, no additional versions are in order—unless the measure is being considered under an innovative "king-of-the-mountain" rule.

On May 21, 1985, for example, the House took up H. Res. 174, providing for consideration of H.R. 1460, the Anti-Apartheid Act of 1985. Under this rule, after completion of the regular amending process, three members could offer their own amendments in the nature of substitutes, one after the other. Each of the three substitutes could be debated for an hour, and each was guaranteed consideration in Committee of the Whole even if members already had agreed to another one of them. If more than one of the substitutes was adopted, only the last to win majority approval would survive the process and be reported back to the House. The manager of the rule, Butler Derrick of South Carolina, explained its unusual provisions:

> House Resolution 174 also provides for the consideration of three substitutes after the bill has been considered for amendment in its entirety. The three substitutes made in order in this rule are those by, and if offered by, Representatives Siljander, Gunderson, and Dellums, and the substitutes must be offered in that sequence.
>
> Mr. Speaker, because the rule makes more than one substitute in order, the rule contains what is sometimes referred to as a king-of-the-hill procedure. Without such a procedure, under the normal rules of the House adoption of an amendment in the nature of a substitute would preclude the offering of any further amendments to the bill. Under the king-of-the-hill procedure provided in this rule, each of the three substitutes can be offered, even if offered subsequent to passage of another substitute. Only the last substitute to be adopted will be reported back to the House.[62]

The germaneness rule was waived to protect the substitutes, which also were protected against second-degree amendments.

Despite its unusual provisions, the rule itself was noncontroversial (only four members voted against it), presumably because everyone's in-

62. *Congressional Record* (May 21, 1985), pp. 12738.

terests were accommodated. The Rules Committee avoided opposition to its rule on such an important and controversial issue; the three members got to offer their own proposals for a South Africa policy; the time of the House was protected because none of the three substitutes could be debated for more than an hour; and the essential policies proposed in the bill were not seriously jeopardized because, when the bill was considered several weeks later and the three substitutes actually were proposed, none of them came within 200 votes of winning.

The Rules Committee was able to achieve much the same objective in much the same way on the following day, May 22, when Derrick called up H. Res 177, the rule for H. Con. Res. 152, the first budget resolution for fiscal year 1986. This rule also proposed a "king-of-the-mountain" procedure by providing for consideration of a sequence of four amendments in the nature of substitutes—for each of them waiving points of order, prohibiting amendments, and allowing an hour of debate—to be offered by three Republican members and a member of the Congressional Black Caucus. Like its predecessor from the day before, H. Res. 177 also assured that each of the substitutes could be offered, no matter what the votes on the preceding ones, and that only the last of them to be adopted, if any, would ultimately be reported back to the House. Although some members opposed the rule for other reasons, no one questioned its "king-of-the-mountain" procedures.[63] But none of the four substitutes attracted more than 102 votes, an outcome that Democratic leaders and their allies on the Rules and Budget committees surely must have anticipated. The true purpose of this rule, then, was not to shape legislative outcomes, but to provide an open and orderly forum for debating a quartet of proposals destined to fail.

As these two examples indicate, "king-of-the-mountain" rules offer the Rules Committee a way of satisfying various factions within the House by allowing them to present their positions and letting the House choose among them. There are few costs associated with such an apparently neutral posture when the Democratic leadership's alternative is sure to win. And when the outcome is less certain, this kind of rule can be designed to give one position an important procedural edge over the others. Consider, for instance, the rules for considering budget resolutions several years earlier, in 1981 and 1982, when the Reagan-induced coalition in the House between Republicans and "Boll Weevil" Democrats was at its peak strength.

The first budget resolution for fiscal year 1982 was considered in April

63. Ibid. (May 22, 1985), pp. 13001–05.

and May 1981 under a "king-of-the-mountain" rule, H. Res. 134, that made in order three amendments in the nature of substitutes, the last of which was to be offered by Delbert Latta, the ranking Republican on the Budget Committee and a member of Rules. During debate on the rule, Republican Robert Walker of Pennsylvania noted that the order in which the rule provided for the substitutes to be offered could "very much make the difference as to how we finally come out on the determination of the House with regard to the budget." That is, by putting the Latta (or Gramm-Latta, as it became known) substitute last in the sequence, "the structure of it probably plays in favor of what the views are of the gentleman from Pennsylvania [Walker] with regard to where we ought to finally end up with the budget."[64] And, in fact, with the 1980 election results fresh in all members' minds, they agreed to the Gramm-Latta amendment, setting in train the subsequent 1981 reconciliation act.

Bolling had responded to Walker that he did not think the order of voting was likely to affect the outcome significantly because he doubted that many members would vote for more than one alternative.[65] In the following year, however, Rules Committee members evidently had the order of voting very much in mind as they drafted H. Res. 477, an extraordinarily complicated rule for considering H. Con. Res. 345, the first budget resolution for fiscal year 1983. Among its many other provisions, the rule allowed three different amendments in the nature of substitutes to be pending simultaneously so that members could amend all three before voting on any of them. But the rule also stated that the last of these substitutes on which the members finally would vote was one to be offered by James Jones, chairman of the Budget Committee, which consisted of the text of H. Con. Res. 345 as the Budget Committee had reported it.

In other words, the Rules Committee so arranged the amending process that members could vote for one or more substitutes for the Budget Committee's proposal, but could then ultimately approve that same proposal by adopting its provisions in the form of the Jones substitute. Yet there was no opposition from the Republican leadership; Trent Lott described the rule as the result of a bipartisan leadership effort "to fashion a fair and equitable approach to this extremely complex issue."[66] Perhaps it is ironic, therefore, that the members were as evenhanded as the committee: they proceeded to reject all three substitutes and then defeated the resolution itself. Nonetheless, the committee had succeeded in de-

64. Ibid. (April 30, 1981), pp. 7993–94.
65. Ibid.
66. Ibid. (May 21, 1982), pp. 11085–93.

vising a rule that satisfied the Republican leadership, by providing for a
vote on its substitute, and the Democratic leadership, by requiring that
the amendment process end with the vote on its preferred alternative.

Self-executing Rules

A second innovation is a recent adaptation of an instrument the Rules
Committee developed for other purposes. In addition to bringing bills to
the floor for initial passage, the committee sometimes is asked to give the
House the opportunity to consider a motion that otherwise could not be
offered—for instance, a motion to concur in Senate amendments to a
House-passed bill before the two houses have gone to conference on it.
To do so, the committee can propose a rule, which is debated under the
one-hour rule, for the consideration of the motion, which is then debated
under the same one-hour rule. But if a majority votes for the rule, that
same majority is virtually certain to vote for the motion as well, leaving
little reason for the House to consider each of them separately. With this
in mind, the committee may report instead what most members know as
a "self-executing" rule, which provides that, by adopting the rule, the
House is deemed also to have taken some other action, such as agreeing
to a motion to concur in Senate amendments.

In an unusual series of developments, for example, the House agreed
to three self-executing rules during the tortuous process of reaching
agreement with the Senate on the Consolidated Omnibus Budget Reconciliation Act of 1985 (COBRA).[67] Two of these rules were H. Res. 330
and H. Res. 390:

> *Resolved,* That upon the adoption of this resolution the House shall
> be considered to have taken from the Speaker's table the bill (H.R.
> 3128) to make changes in spending and revenue provisions for pur-
> poses of deficit reduction and program improvement, consistent
> with the budget process, with the Senate amendments thereto, to
> have agreed to the Senate amendment to the title, to have agreed
> to the Senate amendment to the text with an amendment inserting
> in lieu thereof the texts of the bills H.R. 3128 and H.R. 3500 as
> passed by the House, and to have insisted on said amendment and
> to have requested a conference with the Senate thereon.[68]

67. On this case, see Stanley Bach, "Procedures for Reaching Legislative Agreement: A
Case Study of H.R. 3128, the Consolidated Omnibus Budget Reconciliation Act of 1985,"
report 86-705 GOV (Congressional Research Service, April 15, 1986).

68. H. Res. 330, *Congressional Record* (December 5, 1985), p. 34511.

Resolved, That upon the adoption of this resolution the House shall be considered to have taken from the Speaker's table the bill (II.R. 3128) to provide for reconciliation pursuant to section 2 of the first concurrent resolution on the budget for fiscal year 1986 . . . , with the Senate amendment to the House amendment to the Senate amendment thereto, to have receded from its disagreement to the Senate amendment, and to have concurred in the Senate amendment with an amendment printed in the Congressional Record of March 4, 1986, by Representative Gray of Pennsylvania.[69]

In light of the developments we have already traced, it should not be surprising that the Rules Committee recently has built on precedents such as these and found advantageous opportunities to incorporate self-executing provisions in its rules for considering measures in Committee of the Whole. For example, H.R. 3128, the subject of the two special rules quoted above, initially had been debated and passed on October 31, 1985, under the terms of H. Res. 301, which Representative Derrick described as a modified closed rule. But the only amendments the rule permitted were deemed to be approved by the vote on the rule itself:

No amendment to the bill shall be in order except the following amendments which shall be considered to have been read and *to have been adopted in the House and in the Committee of the Whole*: (1) an amendment to strike out title I of the bill and to insert in lieu thereof the text of H.R. 3290; (2) an amendment printed in the Congressional Record of October 29, 1985, by Representative Rostenkowski of Illinois, relating to single employer plans; and (3) an amendment to the table of contents striking "Medicare program" and inserting in lieu thereof "Health care programs", and inserting at the end of the table of contents "Title VI. Amendments relating to single employer plans."[70]

The first of the three amendments was a compromise among the three committees—Ways and Means, Energy and Commerce, and Judiciary—that shared jurisdiction over these medicare and medicaid proposals. And the second temporarily resolved an ongoing policy disagreement between the Ways and Means and Education and Labor committees. The third amendment was not substantive. In a sense, therefore, this rule created

69. H. Res. 390, ibid. (March 6, 1986), p. 3783.
70. Ibid. (October 31, 1985), p. 29808 (emphasis added).

an intercommittee compromise that was comparable to an alternative substitute. But it went much further; not only did the rule preclude members
from proposing their own amendments, it even prevented them from securing separate, direct votes on the three amendments listed in the rule.
From their perspective, the distinction between a closed rule and a modified closed rule with these self-executing provisions was a distinction
without a difference. As might be expected, therefore, Latta described
H. Res. 301 as "a gag rule," "strictly a take it or leave it proposition," and
urged defeat of the previous question so that he could amend the rule to
permit consideration of five amendments that his Republican colleagues
wished to offer.[71] But the previous question was ordered by a fourteen-
vote margin and the rule then approved by voice vote.

In early December of the same year, the House agreed by voice vote
to another self-executing rule, H. Res. 327, for considering a continuing
resolution for fiscal year 1986. According to Tony Beilenson, Democratic
floor manager of the rule, the time pressures were too great to leave the
joint resolution open to amendment, and it was particularly important to
avoid protracted debate on controversial issues. To this end, the rule included a self-executing provision to strike an abortion provision that Richard Durbin of Illinois had proposed during markup by the Appropriations
Committee as an alternative to one Jack Kemp of New York had offered.
Durbin explained that his amendment was closely related to a law associated with Representative Henry Hyde of Illinois (the so-called Hyde
amendment on abortion funding), but that the Durbin amendment included an inadvertent drafting error. Durbin went on to imply that if he
had sought to offer a floor amendment just to make the needed technical
correction, it might well have opened the entire abortion issue to a long
and contentious debate. So he and Hyde reached an agreement:

> The compromise which we agreed on was as follows: I would
> withdraw my amendment which was offered in the House Commit-
> tee on Appropriations and adopted by a vote of 37 to 16, and the
> gentleman from New York [Mr. Kemp] would not be offering an
> amendment on the floor today. Although Mr. Kemp opposed this
> procedure, the House Committee on Rules did agree to it.[72]

In each of these cases, the Rules Committee played the role of facili-
tator—writing a rule to implement an agreement or resolve a problem
among members or committees that otherwise might have required com-

71. Ibid., pp. 29809–10.
72. Ibid. (December 4, 1985), p. 34139.

mittees to reconvene in scheduled, formal meetings with quorums present. In the process, each rule also protected the agreement against a separate vote on the floor by which members could have rejected it.[73]

Not all self-executing rules have been so innocuous, however, as members learned on December 3, 1987. The House once again needed to pass
a continuing resolution, and the proposed rule for considering it made
room for only ten amendments, three of which were to be adopted via a
self-executing provision.[74] Some normally loyal Democrats joined Republicans in complaining that the Rules Committee had blocked consideration of amendments they advocated. Another source of vocal complaint
was one of the three amendments to be automatically inserted—not offered from the floor and voted on separately—which would have exempted members of Congress (and other senior officials) from a scheduled pay raise. Members were unhappy, but not because they wanted
their salaries to increase. On the contrary, they were frustrated to discover
that the only way they could avoid any taint of association with a pay raise
was to vote for the rule because the rule automatically struck the pay raise
from the continuing resolution.

The opportunity to paint the picture was given to Democrat Jim Chapman of Texas, who recently had found himself at the center of partisan
and procedural controversy for casting the last-minute deciding vote to
pass an omnibus reconciliation bill:

> A few days ago, amidst some rather emotional declarations and
> partisan rhetoric, I cast a vote for the budget reconciliation bill.
> Since that time, my colleagues on the Republican side of the aisle
> have blistered me back in my district and in the press with a line
> that the House of Representatives has increased revenues to give
> itself a raise. . . . Well, today is the day we get to vote to remove
> that pay increase from any legislation that passes the Congress.

73. Two earlier self-executing rules had similar purposes. The 1985 rule for considering
H.R. 1562, a controversial textile trade bill that President Reagan ultimately vetoed, included a self-executing provision for adding an amendment to insert the bill's effective date,
which the Ways and Means Committee had inadvertently omitted. The rule prohibited all
other amendments except Ways and Means Committee amendments. See *Congressional Record* (October 10, 1985), p. 27059. And the self-executing provision of H. Res. 296, adopted
in October 1985 for considering the Omnibus Budget Reconciliation Act, made certain
Banking Committee provisions of the bill subject to annual appropriations. Derrick described the amendment as "primarily technical and clarifying in nature," and "agreeable to
both the Committees on Appropriations and Banking," suggesting that Appropriations may
have requested (or demanded) the amendment to protect its jurisdiction. See *Congressional
Record* (October 23, 1985), p. 28607.

74. Ibid. (December 3, 1987), pp. H10900–11.

As surely as a vote against reconciliation was a vote against the congressional pay raise a few days ago, today a vote against this rule will be a vote for a congressional pay raise, make no mistake about it. Support the rule if you want to strip out the outrageous pay increase.[75]

Chapman became the visible opponent of the pay raise, and members who wanted to oppose the rule were in a quandary. Republican Amory Houghton of New York charged the Rules Committtee with perpetrating "a rather sharp parliamentary trick. . . . If I vote against the rule, I am put into an impossible situation. A vote against the rule could be construed, no matter what the arguments are to the contrary, as a vote to allow a second pay increase for Congress within a 12-month period. I resent that."[76] The House ordered the previous question and adopted the rule by margins of more than fifty votes. Did the pay raise ploy make the difference? We do not know, of course. But we do know that assembling a minimum winning coalition—only the minimal number of votes needed to win—can be a dangerous business. A margin for error is always welcome in a place as unpredictable as the House floor.[77]

As these examples of "king-of-the-mountain" and self-executing rules demonstrate, it is an oversimplification to assert, as Republicans sometimes charge in the heat of debate, that restrictive and complex rules are motivated solely by a quest for partisan advantage. The ways in which the Rules Committee has assisted the Democratic majority have been a principal theme of this study. While pursuing their partisan interests, however, the Democrats as well as the Republicans on Rules also recognize an institutional responsibility. The "king-of-the-mountain" and self-executing provisions we have described generally were not contentious. They were accepted, by and large, as appropriate ways to ratify bipartisan or intercommittee agreements or as useful ways to present an array of alternatives on which members could vote. Yet it is not surprising that Rules Democrats would employ a self-executing rule under much more contentious circumstances when it offered them the most effective means to achieve their end. One should expect no less in a body where political interests and institutional needs coexist.

75. Ibid., p. H10904.
76. Ibid., p. H10906.
77. According to data compiled by Donald Wolfensberger, the number of self-executing rules granted by the Rules Committee jumped markedly during the 99th Congress. He identified a total of eight such rules during the 95th–98th Congresses, but twenty of them during the 99th Congress alone. *Congressional Record*, daily edition (May 24, 1988), p. H3579.

•

Other Arrangements

In emphasizing these two innovations, we do not mean to suggest that they exhaust the range of possibilities the Rules Committee has developed. For instance, some recent rules have contained contingency provisions, under which one amendment may be offered only if another has been rejected. And others have diverged from the normal process of considering amendments to each section or title of a bill in sequence, either by postponing amendments to a portion of the bill until the end of the amending process or by authorizing the chair to decide when a certain title should be open to amendment. Summaries of three of the rules the House adopted during the 99th Congress (1985–86) should suffice to illustrate some of the complicated forms these resolutions now may take.

—H. Res. 222 governed consideration of H.R. 8, the Water Quality Renewal Act of 1985. After providing for the Public Works Committee's substitute to be read for amendment, the resolution stated that the first amendments to it would be a series of amendments, to be considered en bloc, offered by James Howard, chairman of the reporting committee. As chairman, Howard would have been recognized before any other member to offer an amendment, but not to propose a package of amendments that affected portions of the committee substitute that had not yet been read. Moreover, the Rules Committee proposed that:

> If said amendments are adopted, they shall be considered, as finally adopted, to have been adopted in the House and in Committee of the Whole, and it shall be in order to consider the committee amendment in the nature of a substitute, as so modified, as an original bill for the purpose of amendment under the five-minute rule. . . . [78]

In other words, after debating and agreeing to Howard's amendments, members would start the amending process again from the beginning, but now with a new text consisting of the committee's substitute as amended by Howard. No one asked for any explanation of such a strange procedure, nor did anyone ask why the germaneness rule was waived to permit Walter Jones of North Carolina to offer his amendment. Perhaps it had something to do with the fact that Jones was chairman of the Merchant Marine and Fisheries Committee. But all that can be ascertained from the *Congressional Record* is that the House was content to adopt such a rule

78. Ibid. (July 18, 1985), p. 19634.

by voice vote after no more than ten minutes of debate, consisting only of two brief and uninformative statements by Joe Moakley and James Quillen, the floor managers for the Rules Committee. By July 1985, the House evidently had learned to take such rules in stride.

—H. Res. 403 provided for considering H.R. 4332, the Federal Firearms Law Reform Act of 1986. Instead of making the Judiciary Committee's amendment in the nature of a substitute for this gun control bill in order as an original bill for purposes of amendment, as is customary, the rule provided for it to be considered as a first-degree amendment and before any other. Immediately thereafter, Harold Volkmer of Missouri would be recognized to offer a substitute for the Judiciary Committee amendment, so members would be considering two alternative versions of the bill and would be able to amend both of them. But H. Res. 403 also designated Volkmer to be the first one to propose an amendment to his own substitute—something that normally is prohibited by House precedents—so that he could correct a technical drafting error in his amendment as it had been printed in the *Record*. Other members then could offer amendments to either version, but only if their amendments too had already been printed in the *Record*. And the rule also imposed a limit of five hours for considering all amendments, after which members would begin the process of voting on whatever proposals were then pending.

In effect, members could perfect both versions of these gun control amendments and then choose between them by voting on the Volkmer substitute (perhaps as amended by then). But Volkmer's substitute enjoyed an advantage, as Butler Derrick implied when he described the effect of the rule:

> I would note that this rule provides for the full consideration of both proposals. Both proposals are open to the amending process. By operation of this rule, the substitute will be voted on first, as is the normal practice in voting on amendments in the House. Our colleagues will thereby have a straight up-or-down vote on the proposition. If the substitute is defeated, the next vote would occur on the committee amendment, as amended.[79]

To vote for the committee amendment, members first would have to vote against the Volkmer amendment, and, as the debate on the rule indicated, few members expected this to happen. Even supporters of the

79. Ibid. (April 9, 1986), pp. H1645–46.

committee's position evidently thought that their best hope was to amend the Volkmer substitute to make it more palatable. Rules Committee Democrats could have devised a different and even less conventional arrangement that would have benefited their colleagues on Judiciary. In this case, though, the sentiment of the House was clear. By choice or necessity, the committee accommodated it, and only two members voted "nay." [80]

—Finally, H. Res. 541, for considering H.R. 5484, the Omnibus Drug Enforcement, Education, and Control Act of 1985, began by waiving all points of order against consideration of the bill and assigning control of the five hours for general debate to Jim Wright and Robert Michel, the majority and minority leaders, rather than dividing it among the chairmen and ranking members of the twelve House committees that had been involved in developing the bill. The resolution, which the House adopted in September 1986, also included a self-executing provision by which H.R. 5484 was amended by a series of amendments to address what Claude Pepper described as technical drafting errors. The rule then went on to prohibit all other amendments to the bill except for those printed in the Rules Committee's report on the resolution. These amendments included one to be offered by Wright, comprising fourteen separate amendments that other members had requested the committee to make in order, and thirty other amendments, each to be offered by a member designated to do so and only in the order specified in the report. The rule also limited debate on each amendment to the periods of time stated in the report and prohibited amendments to any of the amendments, except for one nongermane perfecting amendment to one of them. Finally, H. Res. 541 denied Republicans the opportunity to offer an additional amendment because it precluded the motion to recommit from containing instructions.

Virtually everyone was satisfied with these arrangements, even though there were at least eighty-eight amendments members had hoped to offer to the bill. Michel described the process of crafting the rule as a bipartisan effort and noted that eighteen of the thirty separate amendments would be proposed by Republicans and that six of the fourteen amendments to

80. In a letter to the authors, Professor Keith Krehbiel observed that Chairman Peter Rodino of the Judiciary Committee actually requested a "king-of-the-mountain" rule for H.R. 4332 during his appearance before the Rules Committee. But the committee rejected the idea after other Democrats characterized Rodino's request as an attempt to gain a strategic advantage by using an "abnormal procedure." In assessing its options in this case, the committee also had to take account of an active effort that was under way to invoke the rarely used discharge rule to bring a special rule for considering the bill directly to the floor.

be offered en bloc by the majority leader had Republican sponsors. James Quillen of the Rules Committee fairly summarized the opinion of the House:

> The rule permits most of the major and many of the less controversial amendments filed with the Rules Committee to be offered. At the same time, it does restrict our ordinary procedures somewhat in the interest of moving this important bill forward expeditiously toward final passage.[81]

In this case, then, the committee sought no partisan advantage and managed to strike a generally acceptable balance between open deliberations and reasonably prompt decisions.

These three rules were not typical, but it has become far harder to characterize any special rule as being typical. Although they may have been unusual, they were not extraordinary by contemporary standards, nor were they the most complicated rules the House adopted during the 99th Congress. And most important, none of them were controversial, though others of their kind certainly were. So far had the Rules Committee and the House come since the mid-1970s.

Conclusion

In this chapter, we have emphasized both adaptation and innovation in special rules. The Rules Committee has adapted to changing conditions and demands in the House by proposing more rules that restrict floor amendments. Whatever other innovative provisions these rules may have included, their primary purpose has been to control and limit the amending process. On the other hand, these provisions have been important in their own right. They too have helped to shape legislative outcomes by defining the alternatives from which members may choose and the strategic context in which their decisions are made. And they are also important for what they reveal about the Rules Committee's approach to its work.

In Congress, politics is neither art nor science, but craft. Using the raw materials available to them, members of the Rules Committee design and construct special rules in the same way that other members create legislation. The products of their labor must be functional, no matter whether they also are Byzantine in their complexity or elegant in their simplicity.

81. *Congressional Record*, daily edition (September 10, 1986), pp. H6519–27.

And just as craftsmen take advantage of or accept the limitations of the natural properties of their raw materials, the Rules Committee attempts to understand all the possibilities, constraints, and nuances associated with the legislation it considers. So while most political metaphors obscure more than they reveal, it is appropriate that members of the House now refer to a process of "crafting" special rules.

Instead of choosing from among a few patterns for its special rules, the Rules Committee has demonstrated a willingness to create unique designs by recombining an increasingly wide array of elements, or by creating new ones as the need arises, to help leaders, committees, and members manage the heightened uncertainties of decisionmaking on the House floor. Not only has the committee become more willing to propose restrictions on amendments, it also has become more adept at crafting these restrictions to promote political or policy objectives—whether it be to compensate for a committee's miscalculation or oversight, protect against a dangerous floor amendment, or tilt the outcome of a choice among alternatives.

CHAPTER FOUR

Evolving Attitudes and Changing Expectations

WE HAVE ARGUED that the trend toward more restrictive rules represented a process of adaptation by the Rules Committee in cooperation with the majority party leadership. In the late 1970s, reliance on restrictive provisions in special rules emerged as a recognized strategy to manage the uncertainties and dangers of decisionmaking on the House floor. In the 1980s, once this practice had become established, restrictive rules came to be used with even more tactical calculation and in more refined and varied ways, as the Rules Committee adapted its innovation to respond more creatively to circumstances and needs that differed from one measure to the next.

The new pattern of special rules could not have been imposed on the House against its will and would not have been possible if most members of the House had not been prepared to accept it. As one would expect, therefore, the changing nature of Rules Committee decisions has been accompanied and made possible by the emergence of a set of widely shared views about the use of restrictive rules—certainly among Democrats, but to a lesser extent among Republicans as well.

Members' Expectations

An early turning point in members' attitudes toward the use of restrictive rules appears to have come with the special rule for considering the 1977 energy bill, a controversial multiple-committee measure by which the House responded to President Carter's energy proposals.[1] This massive

1. For background on this episode, see Stanley Bach, "Complexities of the Legislative Process: A Case Study of Congressional Consideration of National Energy Legislation During the 95th Congress," report 79-68 GOV (Congressional Research Service, March 7, 1979); and Bruce I. Oppenheimer, "Policy Effects of U.S. House Reform: Decentralization and

bill and the energy crisis provoking it posed particularly delicate problems for House Democratic leaders, who knew that it would create cross-cutting divisions along partisan, regional, and jurisdictional lines. Speaker O'Neill responded by appointing, with House approval, an ad hoc committee to consolidate and integrate the proposals of five standing committees to which parts of the package were referred, a step that helped the leadership build a majority coalition for the bill. However, the tentative character of support for the package, especially from many Democrats, left party leaders concerned that the ties holding the coalition together would unravel under the irresistible tug of unfriendly floor amendments. In reaction, the Rules Committee proposed H. Res. 727, limiting amendments other than those reported by the ad hoc committee to twelve designated floor amendments, including a Republican amendment in the nature of a substitute. In the view of O'Neill's top legislative aide, Democratic leaders' satisfaction with this rule led them to think about proposing restrictive rules for other legislation, in addition to the tax bills and the few other matters for which such rules had been reserved in the past.[2]

The floor debate on H. Res. 727 touched on several themes that would recur in debates on restrictive rules in years to come. As the majority floor manager for the Rules Committee, Richard Bolling offered this explanation of the amending process under the rule:

> The process is restrictive, but an effort was made to be as fair as possible on the major issue. For example, there will be a vote on the very controversial question of to regulate or not to regulate natural gas. . . .
>
> I believe this rule is fair, because in the process of considering it the Committee on Rules decided to include additional amendments that had not originally been thought probable to be considered. The Committee on Rules provided also to the minority not only a motion to recommit with or without instructions, but also a substitute at the end of the bill.
>
> When the rule was reported, it was reported by a voice vote, and I do not believe significant objection was heard. The ranking member of the committee . . . described the rule as fair in his discussion,

---

the Capacity to Resolve Energy Issues," *Legislative Studies Quarterly*, vol. 5 (February 1980), pp. 5–30.

2. Interview on July 19, 1987, with Ari Weiss, formerly executive director of the Democratic Steering and Policy Committee.

although he did indicate that he would obviously have preferred an open rule.[3]

Several of Bolling's defenses have become familiar themes on the House floor: though the rule was restrictive, important issues were the subjects of floor amendments; the Rules Committee had been responsive to members' requests; and the interests of the minority party were protected by an opportunity to propose a substitute version of the bill, as well as by its right under House rules to offer a motion to recommit with instructions.

The Republican reaction to H. Res. 727 also set the tone and themes that the minority often would adopt in similar situations during the following decade. The criticisms by John Anderson of Illinois and Del Clawson of California, speaking from opposite ideological wings of the Republican party, touched the core of rank-and-file Republican opposition to restrictive rules.[4] While some of the amendments protected by the rule had Republican sponsors, Anderson expressed the frustration shared by many of his fellow partisans who sought additional opportunities to offer amendments:

> Our appeals for a little more fairness, a little more openness, a little more balance, always seem to fall on deaf ears on the other side of the aisle. In short, we are stuck with the futility and frustration of being in the minority under a procedure such as this.
>
> Majority rule does not mean domination by the majority party leadership, or even by the majority party caucuses of the various committees. It means the free exercise of judgment by a majority of the Members of Congress.[5]

Anderson's two comments begin to reveal some of the ambivalence that would come to characterize Republican reactions to restrictive rules, as he first appealed for "a little more fairness . . . a little more balance," but then implied that any restriction on floor amendments unjustly limits members' right to participate in the legislative process.

The opportunity for the minority to offer a substitute for the ad hoc committee's version of the bill did not satisfy many Republicans, as Clawson argued:

3. *Congressional Record* (July 29, 1977), pp. 25654–55.
4. See Robert E. Bauman, "Majority Tyranny in the House," in John H. Rousselot and Richard T. Schulze, eds., *View from the Capital Dome (Looking Right)* (Ottawa, Ill.: Green Hill Publishers, 1980).
5. *Congressional Record* (July 29, 1977), pp. 25655–56.

Allowing the Republican substitute was meaningless. It was not even a sop, in my opinion, to allow the minority to offer its amendment in the form of a substitute, because it is not about to be accepted.[6]

The Republicans wanted more than the chance to present their alternative and force a vote on it. Many of them evidently believed that their substitute had little chance of being adopted, because the vote on it would be perceived as a partisan issue. But they also thought that there were Democratic members who would support some of their proposals if they were offered individually. So to these Republicans, the Rules Committee's apparent gesture of evenhandedness was really nothing more than a clever way of dooming their prospects of amending the ad hoc committee's package on the floor.

Over the course of the period between 1975 and 1986, such contentions were heard over and over again, as restrictive rules were debated on the House floor with increasing frequency. More and more members also came to share Anderson and Clawson's understanding that the outcomes of seemingly procedural votes on special rules could have enormous policy consequences, and that these votes put Republicans at a marked disadvantage. But arguments about arcane parliamentary procedures seldom make good political capital, as House Republican leader Robert Michel explained:

Nothing is so boring to the layman as a litany of complaints over the more obscure provisions of House procedures. It is all "inside baseball." Even among the media, none but the brave seek to attend to the howls of dismay from Republicans over such esoterica as the kinds of rules under which we are forced to debate. But what is more important to a democracy than the method by which its laws are created?

We Republicans are all too aware that when we laboriously compile data to demonstrate the abuse of legislative power by the Democrats, we are met by reporters and the public with that familiar symptom best summarized in the acronym "MEGO"—my eyes glaze over. We can't help it if the battles of Capitol Hill are won or lost before the issues get to the floor by the placement of an amendment or the timing of a vote. We have a voice and a vote to fight the disgraceful manipulation of the rules by the Democrats, and we

6. Ibid., p. 25658.

make use of both. All we need now is media attention, properly directed to those boring, but all-important, House procedures.[7]

During the last decade, standing committees frequently have requested restrictive rules for their controversial bills and, as we have shown, the Rules Committee often has granted them. By the time the 100th Congress convened in 1987, most members probably had come to expect that the committee would propose special rules with restrictive provisions for considering all substantively complex and politically difficult bills. In a recent interview, one Democratic Rules member stated flatly, "When there is much controversy involved, some sort of limit on amendments is usually considered."[8] In fact, some Rules members have even asserted that the committee is quite generous in proposing open rules as often as they do—roughly half the time. And as Michel's lament suggests, when Rules Democrats have proposed restrictive rules for partisan advantage, they have had little reason to fear that they would have to contend with adverse public reactions or electoral repercussions.

As members have learned to expect restrictive rules for major bills, they have had to adjust their own behavior. No longer can members who want to offer amendments to such a bill simply wait for it to come to the floor. If they do, they risk discovering that the bill is going to be considered under a rule that precludes them from proposing their amendments. So members must anticipate this possibility by seeking information about the kind of rule the committee of jurisdiction has requested, consulting with Rules members or staff before the committee's formal hearing to gauge its intentions, making timely requests to testify at the hearing, and attempting to convince Rules that their amendments should be among those favored for consideration. And they must protect themselves in this way even if their amendments do not require waivers to protect them against points of order.

Inevitably, many members fail to take these steps, perhaps because they are not yet accustomed to looking far enough ahead. It is particularly difficult for members to pay attention to the progress and prospects of bills being reported by House committees on which they do not serve and to examine such bills with care, even consulting with constituents and district officials about local effects and implications in order to decide

7. Robert H. Michel, "The Minority Leader Replies," *Washington Post*, December 29, 1987, p. A14.
8. Anonymous interview with one of the authors.

whether to prepare one or more amendments to them.[9] So restrictive rules undoubtedly have precluded floor consideration of some amendments merely because the Rules Committee did not receive timely requests to make them in order. The Democratic Caucus recognized this potential problem in 1973 when it established its procedure for instructing the Democrats on Rules to make certain amendments in order. At the same time, the caucus agreed that no committee chairman should seek a rule prohibiting any germane amendment until four days after giving notice in the *Record* of his or her intention. But restrictive provisions now have become so frequent and widely accepted that this requirement sometimes is ignored.[10]

When Rules Committee members draft restrictive rules, they usually find themselves in the uncomfortable position of choosing which of their colleagues' amendments to send to, or bar from, the floor. In confronting these decisions more frequently in recent years, Rules members have developed opinions about how to make the necessary choices—opinions that are still in the process of crystallizing into norms. The committee's Democratic majority frequently identifies which amendments warrant floor consideration in a consensus-building process in the days and hours before formal Rules Committee meetings.[11] While Rules members stress

9. This is one respect in which informal congressional caucuses can be useful—by creating a network of members with shared interests or positions who can keep each other informed with timely reports about developments occurring throughout the House committee system.

10. The caucus procedure for instructing the Democrats on Rules also has fallen into disuse. Once the Rules Committee began to think in terms of restrictive rules and the Speaker received authority to nominate its Democratic members, it became much less likely that the committee would fail to provide for an amendment that most Democrats supported, if for no other reason than the committee's natural desire to avoid having its special rules defeated on the floor.

11. It became standard practice for Rules Committee Democrats to meet even before their formal hearing on a bill to decide on the basic framework, and often the precise terms, of the rule they would approve. Although this practice continues, participants report that especially during the 99th Congress more decisions were actually made during Rules Committee hearings and markups. If so, this development probably reflected the attitude of Speaker O'Neill and the retirement of Chairman Bolling and may not prove to be a lasting change in practice, depending on the long-term relationship that develops between Speaker Wright and the committee. In any event, advance decisionmaking by the Rules Committee's majority is hardly a new, or a Democratic party, phenomenon. George Rothwell Brown speaks of Speaker Reed in the days when he chaired the committee and appointed the two Democrats and two other Republicans who served with him: "It was his custom, when he and McKinley and Cannon agreed upon a program, and Carlisle and Randall had appeared in the Speaker's room, to extend the typewritten special rule which had been agreed upon and say with grim sarcasm, 'Gentlemen, we have decided to perpetrate the following out-

the case-by-case nature of their approach, they have developed impre-
cise, fluid guidelines about the kinds of amendments that deserve a hearing on the floor. Some committee members characterize these amendments as "legitimate"; the special rules making them in order are "fair."

Rules Committee members and staff, both Democrats and Republicans, mention several criteria for assessing a prospective amendment in
addition to the public policy it proposes: the committee and subcommittee position of the sponsor, the clarity and precision with which it is
drafted, its prospects for adoption on the floor, and the past history of the
amendment—any action taken on it or similar proposals earlier during
the Congress or in previous Congresses. Thus a well-drafted amendment
that is to be proposed by a subcommittee or committee member, that had
been narrowly defeated during markup, and that many House members
are presumed to support is most likely to be perceived as legitimate. It
would only be fair to allow the amendment's sponsor to appeal his or her
loss in committee by offering the amendment on the floor, where all
members deserve the chance to consider it. And as we discussed in chapter 3, the Rules Committee has demonstrated a marked bias in favor of
amendments by committee members, who presumably are most familiar
with the legislation and the issues it raises.

Not surprisingly, Republicans have been less comfortable with, and
less likely to share in, any emerging Democratic consensus about when
restrictive rules are appropriate and what constitutes a fair restrictive rule.
Trent Lott of Mississippi, as the Republican whip as well as a senior
member of Rules, frequently spoke out against restrictions on amending
activity, particularly as they affected amendments that rank-and-file Republicans would offer. He charged, for example, that "the Democratic
leadership is trying to turn the Rules Committee into the stranglehold on
this institution that it was 30 years ago." [12] But Republicans have not consistently opposed restrictive rules, especially for bills reported from committee with bipartisan support. In such cases, the reporting committee's
minority members may find themselves torn between a commitment to a
compromise they had reached in committee and their interest in protecting the rights and interests of fellow Republicans. And when Republicans

---

rage.' In this bold and perfectly brazen manner would the minority be informed of the
purpose of the majority leaders to pass a bill, of however much importance, under a special
rule. . . ." George Rothwell Brown, *The Leadership of Congress* (Indianapolis: Bobbs-Merrill,
1922), p. 88.

12. Janet Hook, "GOP Chafes Under Restrictive House Rules," *Congressional Quarterly
Weekly Report*, vol. 45 (October 10, 1987), p. 2449.

have sought to substitute their own proposal for a rule, it usually has been a different package of restrictions, which, they argue, would present the House with a fairer and more complete set of choices—including, of course, Republican amendments the Rules Committee had excluded.

Norms of fairness and legitimacy are liable to be strained at the end of a session, when time constraints become severe and there is the greatest incentive for the committee to be most selective. For example, when the rule for a bill to shore up the agricultural credit system came to the floor in September 1987, the Democratic floor manager asserted:

> Mr. Speaker, the Rules Committee is also very aware of the increasing demand for floor time as the session comes to a close. Therefore, with the urgency of this bill and the need to make good use of floor time both in mind, the Rules Committee crafted this rule which deals with this bill expeditiously while allowing great latitude and flexibility in the amendments that can be offered.[13]

Compared with many recent rules, this resolution was quite generous in allowing thirty-nine floor amendments, but it did bar second-degree amendments and limited the debate to ten minutes on each amendment, regardless of its importance. In general, the pressures in the last few weeks of a session increase the costs of delays on the floor and the dangers of uncertainty about likely floor decisions and so lead to more restrictive special rules that are more likely to be more acceptable to the House.

Restrictive rules also seem more acceptable, and their strategic effect more widely recognized, when the bill or resolution to be considered is an omnibus measure, such as the 1977 energy package and the various reconciliation, tax, and continuing appropriations measures of the 1980s. Packaging many diverse proposals into a single, massive, complex, and controversial vehicle can have several advantages to committees and leaders, not the least of which is the likelihood that it will receive a restrictive rule. The sheer magnitude of these bills, combined with the time pressures under which they often are considered, is a powerful argument against considering them under open rules. Thus one of the reasons House committee leaders tolerated the use of reconciliation bills in the early 1980s was because these bills enabled committees to send some controversial and largely extraneous provisions, such as program reauthorizations, to the floor under special rules giving them more protection

13. *Congressional Record*, daily edition (September 21, 1987), p. H7638.

against amendments than they otherwise could have expected to obtain.[14] Committee leaders accepted unusual limitations on their discretion in return for the benefit of restrictive rules. By the same token, there can be an advantage in incorporating a controversial appropriations bill, such as for foreign assistance, in a continuing resolution, rather than bringing it to the House floor as one of the thirteen annual appropriations bills. While these separate bills almost always are fully open to amendment, continuing resolutions are much more likely to be considered under restrictive or even closed rules. And anticipating this prospect, the chairmen of other House committees may withhold their authorization bills from the floor, preferring to work with their colleagues on Appropriations to incorporate necessary changes in existing law as part of the continuing resolution.

In short, the recent trends in special rules have affected committee recommendations and leadership strategies as well as opportunities for individual members to amend bills on the floor. Over the past decade, members, senior staff, and other participants in the legislative struggle have had to become students of the larger repertoire of provisions from which the Rules Committee now selects as it assembles the pieces of its special rules. They can even learn to expect certain combinations of provisions in recurring legislative situations or for particular kinds of measures such as budget resolutions. Moreover, there is slowly beginning to develop, among House Democrats at least, a prevailing view of the appropriate uses of restrictive rules. Even though there is no agreement on such a controversial question, and certainly nothing resembling a bipartisan consensus, Rules Committee members have become quite adept at calculating what restrictions the House will tolerate when they bring their special rules to the floor.

Voting on Special Rules

House support for special rules, restrictive or otherwise, is inextricably entangled with the distribution and intensity of members' policy preferences concerning the measures to be considered. Unfortunately, we can only examine what procedural arrangements a majority of representatives have supported, not what they would have supported; we cannot compare what they have found acceptable with what they would have considered

14. See Steven S. Smith, *Call to Order: Floor Politics in the House and Senate* (Brookings, forthcoming), chap. 3.

optimal. Nonetheless, the House's reactions to the special rules the Rules Committee has proposed in recent years yield some important insights into the ways in which the relationships among the committee, the two parties, and the House as a whole have changed in this new era of restrictive rules.

Members who oppose a special rule have two principal options for challenging it on the floor. First, they can attempt to defeat the rule itself, but doing so typically prevents the bill at issue from reaching the floor for consideration, unless and until Rules reports a second, more palatable rule. Alternatively, they may seek to amend the proposed rule on the floor so that the House can consider the measure but under a different set of procedural ground rules. To do so, they must first convince a majority to defeat the motion to order the previous question, which the Democratic floor manager invariably makes during or at the end of the first hour of debate on the rule. If adopted, this motion concludes the debate, precludes all amendments to the rule, and normally leads immediately to the vote on adopting it. But if a majority does not vote to order the previous question, an opponent of the rule as reported then is recognized for an hour, during which he or she can offer an amendment to it. The motion to order the previous question is not debatable. So whenever members seek to defeat this motion, they must explain their intention and their reasons, and the amendment they would propose if successful, during the first hour of debate on the rule itself, before the motion is made.

An amendment to a special rule must be germane to it, just like any other amendment to any other measure. Under House precedents, for instance, an amendment to a simple open rule would be considered nongermane to the rule if it proposed to waive a point of order to permit a member to offer a floor amendment that was not germane to the bill to which the rule applied.[15] While the Rules Committee may craft a rule that permits consideration of a nongermane amendment to a bill by including such a waiver, a floor amendment to the rule having the same effect would not be in order under most circumstances. When the amendment that opponents of a rule would propose is nongermane, therefore, they may adopt a third option: encouraging the House to defeat the pre-

15. See *Congressional Record* (May 29, 1980), p. 12673; and Stanley Bach, "The Structure of Choice in the House of Representatives: The Impact of Complex Special Rules," *Harvard Journal on Legislation*, vol. 18 (Summer 1981), pp. 601–02. It is interesting to note that the germaneness of amendments to special rules did not become an issue and the subject of precedent-setting rulings until recently, when restrictive rules often divided the House along party lines.

vious question so they can then move to refer the rule back to the Rules Committee. But this option has been pursued in only a handful of instances since the mid-1970s.[16]

The key vote on a special rule comes on ordering the previous question when the rule's opponents object to its terms, not to taking up the bill it would make in order. But if members oppose considering a bill under any parliamentary circumstances, they may agree by voice vote to ordering the previous question, and then demand a roll call vote on adopting the rule itself. In addition, Republican members sometimes require a roll call on adoption not with any expectation of, or even real interest in, defeating the rule, but as a way of registering a protest against the restrictions the committee and a majority of the House are imposing on them. If the previous question is ordered by roll call vote, however, it is relatively unusual for members to require a roll call on adoption as well.

It is reasonable to expect that the movement toward more restrictive rules would produce more floor challenges to Rules Committee proposals, and the most obvious manifestation of such challenges would be an increase in demands for roll call votes on the previous question or adoption. Indeed, as table 4-1 reveals, roughly half of all special rules stimulated a roll call during most of the Congresses we are examining.[17] On the previous question, the frequency of roll call votes increased after the 94th Congress (1975–76), as the percentage of complicated and restrictive special rules also began to rise. The 99th Congress (1985–86) is especially noteworthy: more than 60 percent of special rules were subject to a roll call, nearly 10 percent faced a relatively close vote, and almost 8 percent were challenged by a roll call vote on the previous question.

In view of the recognized importance of special rules and the controversy that often surrounds them, it is striking that only during the most recent Congresses were even 9 percent of all rules subject to a contested roll call vote in which the majority prevailed by a three-to-two margin or less. The outcome of roll calls on special rules, whether on the previous question or on adoption, generally has not been in serious doubt. During the 97th-99th Congresses (1981–86), the House defeated the previous question and amended rules only twice, both times in the 97th Congress: to consider Gramm-Latta II, the Reagan-led conservative coalition pro-

---

16. If the House does vote to refer, the Rules Committee is likely to react by proposing a different rule that it hopes will attract more support, but there is no assurance that the new rule will take the form the committee's opponents had advocated on the floor.

17. The frequency of roll call votes on special rules was unaffected by the advent of recorded voting in Committee of the Whole because special rules are considered in the full House.

TABLE 4-1. Characteristics of Voting on Special Rules, 94th–99th Congresses (1975–86)[a]

Percent

	Congress					
Characteristic	94th ('75–'76)	95th ('77–'78)	96th ('79–'80)	97th ('81–'82)	98th ('83–'84)	99th ('85–'86)
Percent of rules subject to any roll call vote	42.7	55.9	45.9	33.7	39.2	61.4
Percent of rules subject to a contested vote[b]	2.8	4.3	6.6	6.7	9.6	9.9
Votes on previous question						
Percent of rules subject to roll call vote	2.8	5.9	5.5	3.8	5.6	7.9
Mean percent of Democrats voting "nay"	17.9	25.6	26.5	49.2	4.6	7.3
Mean percent of Republicans voting "nay"	99.5	63.5	81.2	32.0	92.9	86.5
Partisanship[c]	81.6	37.9	54.7	17.2	88.3	79.2
Votes on adoption						
Percent of rules subject to roll call vote	40.7	52.7	43.1	33.7	38.4	58.4
Mean percent of Democrats voting "nay"	5.2	4.7	5.5	9.7	7.1	6.0
Mean percent of Republicans voting "nay"	14.9	19.7	28.9	34.5	47.3	42.3
Partisanship[c]	9.7	15.0	23.4	24.8	40.2	36.3

a. This table presents data only on special rules for initial floor consideration of measures, but not rules solely or primarily for waiving points of order for general appropriations measures.

b. Contested votes are those on which the margin of victory was 60–40 or closer.

c. Partisanship is the mean absolute difference between the percentage of Republicans voting "nay" and the percentage of Democrats voting "nay."

posal for the 1981 reconciliation bill, and an "airport and airway improvement" bill.[18] (In each case, the Republicans' substitute rule was restrictive.) And only six rules were rejected during the same period. These data are a useful reminder that the legislative business the House transacts on the floor is far more often routine than contentious.[19]

Successful challenges to special rules may have been just frequent enough to keep Rules Democrats and the majority leadership attentive to the preferences of the House as a whole. Not surprisingly, restrictive

18. H. Res. 489, amended and adopted on July 23, 1982.

19. A roll call vote on a rule does not always indicate that it has caused serious controversy. When the House is expected to begin debating a bill immediately after adopting the rule for considering it, a roll call vote on the rule serves the same purpose as a quorum call and notifies all members that the bill is about to be called up.

TABLE 4-2. Mean Number of "Nay" Votes on Roll Calls to Adopt
Special Rules, by Type of Rule, 94th–99th Congresses (1975–86)

Type of special rule	Congress					
	94th ('75–'76)	95th ('77–'78)	96th ('79–'80)	97th ('81–'82)	98th ('83–'84)	99th ('85–'86)
Open	23.1	24.5	27.4	30.1	44.6	64.0
Restrictive	77.6	92.6	99.7	143.5	146.4	100.3
Closed	63.2	79.0	145.2	117.6	122.7	128.8
Number of roll call votes on adopting special rules	101	98	78	35	48	59

and closed rules have engendered more controversy and conflict than
open rules, as table 4-2 demonstrates. Except for the 99th Congress
(1985–86), there were more than three times as many votes, on average,
against adopting restrictive rules than against open rules. In fact, between
1977 and 1986, all the special rules that produced a contested vote restricted floor amendments to some degree, and all six of the rules defeated between 1981 and 1986 were restrictive rules for considering controversial bills.[20] But the vast majority of all rules—open, restrictive, and
closed rules alike—have not been in serious jeopardy on roll call votes.

The Rules Committee's success on the floor undoubtedly reflects the
ability of its members to understand the preferences and anticipate the
reactions of their colleagues. Yet the frequency (or infrequency) of contested roll calls on special rules, and the rarity with which rules have been
amended or rejected, tell only part of the story about how the House has
reacted to the procedural ground rules the committee has proposed. Table
4-2 also indicates that all types of rules, even open rules, confronted more
"nay" votes on adoption in the 1980s than in the 1970s. This poses a small
puzzle. The consistently higher levels of opposition to restrictive and
closed rules are not surprising; they only document the fact that limits on
amending opportunities alienate some members. But why should all
types of rules have bred more opposition in recent years than in the
1970s? The answer lies in the changing pattern of partisan opposition.

Sources of Partisan Opposition

The character of voting on special rules has changed dramatically, even
though the outcomes have not. In particular, roll call votes on adopting

20. It bears repeating that, for purposes of this discussion, "restrictive" rules include all
rules with restrictive provisions, even those with a combination of other provisions that led
us to classify them as "complex" for purposes of table 3-2 and the related discussion.

TABLE 4-3. Partisanship in Roll Call Votes on Adopting Special Rules,
94th–99th Congresses (1975–86)

Percent

	Congress					
Degree of partisanship[a]	94th ('75–'76)	95th ('77–'78)	96th ('79–'80)	97th ('81–'82)	98th ('83–'84)	99th ('85–'86)
Low (0–25)	83.2	73.5	65.4	57.1	39.6	44.1
Moderate (26–50)	9.9	17.3	10.3	17.1	12.5	15.3
High (51–75)	4.0	9.2	12.8	17.1	16.7	30.5
Very high (76–100)	3.0	0	11.5	8.6	31.3	10.2

a. Partisanship is the mean absolute difference between the percentage of Republicans voting "nay" and the percentage of Democrats voting "nay."

rules have shown a striking increase in partisanship since the late 1970s. Table 4-1 indicates that the gap between the percentage of Republicans opposing rules on adoption and the percentage of Democrats doing so has expanded greatly in the 1980s. On average, the difference was roughly twice as great during the 98th–99th Congresses (1983–86) as it had been during the three previous Congresses (1977–82). The source of the change, table 4-1 also makes plain, has been declining support for special rules among Republicans. In only one of the Congresses between 1975 and 1986, the turbulent 97th, did more than 8 percent of the Democrats, on average, vote against adoption of special rules. But the level of Republican opposition grew markedly during the same period, roughly tripling between the 94th Congress and the 98th and 99th Congresses. Even on average, almost half of the Republicans voted against adoption during the 98th and 99th Congresses.

The mean values for partisanship in table 4-1 are not deceiving. As table 4-3 illustrates, the shift to more partisan voting is not due to a few extreme cases, but rather reflects a general increase in partisan differences on adoption votes. As recently as the 96th Congress, only one-third of the votes on adopting rules produced interparty differences of more than 25 percent; in the 98th and 99th Congresses, by contrast, two-fifths of the roll call votes on agreeing to rules yielded differences of more than 50 percent. When seven of eight Democrats vote for a resolution and seven of eight Republicans vote against it, the result is a partisanship score of 75 percent; in the 98th Congress, a remarkable 31 percent of adoption votes demonstrated this high degree of partisan polarization.

The effect of ordering the previous question suggests that there should be even more dramatic evidence of partisan differences on roll call votes on these motions. Opposition to special rules usually is led by the minority floor manager, who can use the debate time he controls to argue that the reported rule is deficient and to expound on the virtues of the amendment he intends to propose if a majority of members vote against ordering the previous question. So demands for roll call votes on the previous question almost always come from the Republican side of the aisle, usually when the minority is fairly well united in opposition to the proposed rule, and often follow criticisms that the Democrats have acted unreasonably or unfairly. The result is a choice that typically is defined in partisan terms and results in highly partisan votes. As table 4-1 indicates, the levels of partisanship on previous question votes are consistently and markedly higher than the partisan differences on adoption votes. Against the background of this pattern, the partisanship scores for the 98th and 99th Congresses stand out and document intense interparty conflict. The unity of both parties on previous question votes during these years was remarkable indeed, reaching levels that would satisfy even the leaders of most parliamentary parties.[21]

The partisan pattern of voting on special rules underscores the weakness of Republican support for the criteria that have been evolving among Democrats to govern the design of restrictive rules. But the minority party has not routinely and consistently opposed the restrictive and closed rules the Rules Committee has reported. While some Republicans have claimed to oppose limitations on amending activity on principle, as indefensible constraints on their constitutional rights as legislators, most of them have demonstrated a willingness to tolerate restrictive rules in some circumstances. At one time or another, most Republicans have acknowledged the need or even expressed a preference for a rule to restrict amendments in order to organize floor debate, enhance the predictability of the floor schedule, and expedite consideration and final passage of important or complex legislation. In 1982, for example, former Minority Leader John Rhodes, then serving on the Rules Committee, disagreed with some of his party colleagues about the merits of a highly complex and restrictive rule for considering a budget resolution. Rhodes argued:

> I feel a greater sense of urgency as far as time is concerned, I guess, than most people do, in getting this done. I do feel that we will have done a deed which we should have learned 3 or 4 years ago

21. The data we are presenting are only for the special rules that the House adopted as proposed by the Rules Committee. Although only a few rules were amended or rejected, this and other tables do not take these instances into account.

TABLE 4 4. Mean Percentage of "Nay" Votes on Roll Calls to Adopt
Special Rules, by Type of Rule and Party, 94th–99th Congresses
(1975–86)

Type of rule and party	Congress					
	94th ('75–'76)	95th ('77–'78)	96th ('79–'80)	97th ('81–'82)	98th ('83–'84)	99th ('85–'86)
Open						
Democrat	3.3	2.6	3.4	3.3	1.2	3.1
Republican	11.4	13.3	13.8	14.5	28.6	34.0
Restrictive						
Democrat	12.7	12.9	9.2	16.7	13.2	9.9
Republican	33.0	43.1	53.8	59.3	71.8	46.5
Closed						
Democrat	15.1	8.7	11.6	16.3	14.3	5.6
Republican	22.0	43.4	78.2	47.3	55.8	68.2

when this budget process took approximately 2 weeks to finish because of the fact that we were dealing with line item amendments.[22]

As table 4-4 indicates, restrictive and even closed rules sometimes have
received substantial Republican support. Only in the 98th Congress did
more than 60 percent of the Republicans, on average, vote against restrictive rules. In the next Congress, average Republican opposition fell to
less than 47 percent.

Republican reactions to restrictive special rules have been related to
the ways and extent to which these rules have proposed to limit the
amending process. In the 98th and 99th Congresses (1983–86), the level
of Republican opposition to special rules that limited floor amendments
(to those specified in the rule itself or the accompanying Rules Committee report) tended to increase as the degree of restrictiveness increased.
On average, nearly four-fifths of the House Republicans voted against
adopting rules that permitted only one amendment to be offered, while
more than half the Republicans supported rules allowing five or more
amendments. So there is some relationship between the restrictiveness
of special rules and the extent of Republican opposition to them. But
restrictive special rules have provoked significant levels of Republican
opposition (40 percent or more) even when the rules permitted members
to offer as many as eleven or more floor amendments.

One also might expect more unified Republican opposition to restrictive rules that permit amendments to be offered only by Democrats or

22. *Congressional Record* (May 21, 1982), p. 11088.

members of the committee of origin. However, our data fail to document any such straightforward relationships. The extent of Republican opposition actually was significantly greater for rules allowing only *Republican* amendments than for rules permitting only Democratic amendments. And Republican opposition was almost as great for rules that made in order only amendments by noncommittee members as for those allowing amendments only by members of the committee (or committees) of jurisdiction.[23]

These counterintuitive patterns probably are attributable to the fact that special rules providing only for Republican amendments usually have limited them severely, to one or two amendments to be offered by senior committee Republicans. Of the ten rules permitting only Republican amendments during the 98th and 99th Congresses, six made in order only one amendment sponsored by a committee Republican, and three others allowed two, three, and four amendments, but all to be offered by committee Republicans. The measures to which these rules related also are noteworthy. Three of the ten rules were for considering budget resolutions or continuing resolutions, and the others addressed such controversial programs and issues as Superfund, arms control compliance, medicaid, and the trade act. On measures of such political and policy significance, the Democrats evidently were anxious to limit amending activity, but also concerned to protect themselves against charges that they were foreclosing consideration of Republican proposals. So the Rules Committee was careful to permit a vote on at least one Republican amendment, which sometimes was an alternative version of the entire bill.[24] Because the vote on the amendment would be cast clearly in partisan terms, however, Rules Committee Democrats could be confident that they were not putting the committee's position at serious risk.[25]

23. On average, 67 percent of the Republicans voting opposed rules providing only for amendments sponsored by Democrats, and 55 percent voted against rules permitting amendments sponsored by members of both parties, while fully 83 percent opposed rules providing only for Republican amendments. Also on average, 78 percent of the Republicans voted against rules providing only for amendments sponsored by members of the reporting committee, compared with 76 percent who opposed rules that made in order only amendments to be proposed by members not on the reporting committee and 39 percent who opposed rules permitting amendments sponsored by committee and noncommittee members.

24. Had the Rules Committee and the House agreed to a closed rule instead in such cases, the Republicans might still have been able to present their alternative through a motion to recommit with instructions. If so, making a germane Republican alternative in order as an amendment may have amounted to little more than recognizing an inevitability.

25. In only one of the ten cases was the Republican amendment adopted on the floor, and that was to the measure of least national or partisan significance, a bill pertaining to the Columbia River Gorge.

In the kinds of cases we have just been discussing, of course, minority party members objected to both the content of the measures and the restrictiveness of the rules for considering them. Indeed, we have no way to separate Republicans' opposition on procedural grounds from their opposition on substantive grounds. Partisan votes on rules are followed, more often than not, by partisan votes on measures. During the 98th and 99th Congresses, ninety-four rules were subject to party votes—in which a majority of Democrats opposed a majority of Republicans—on the previous question, adoption, or both. In more than three cases out of four, these votes were followed by party votes in connection with the measures the rules made in order—on an amendment, final passage, or both. Unfortunately, we cannot say, for example, to what extent Republican "nay" votes on rules were provoked by their opposition to the bills at issue, nor can we gauge if and when less restrictive rules would have resulted in less party voting on amendments and bills. Disentangling procedure and policy in the House is as difficult for purposes of analysis as for purposes of practical politics on the floor.[26]

That we have found more partisan voting on restrictive and closed rules than on open rules is predictable enough. But increasing party differences are not merely a consequence of increasing proportions of restrictive rules. As table 4-4 indicates, there generally have been larger differences between the two parties' voting patterns in recent years than in the mid-1970s for open rules as well as for restrictive rules. And, for each type of rule, greater Republican opposition has been at the core of the trend toward greater partisan disagreement. Clearly, then, the increasing, and increasingly partisan, controversy over special rules cannot be attributed entirely to Republican disagreements with restrictive rules.

One evident cause of partisan controversy over open as well as restrictive and closed rules has been the increasing frequency with which the resolutions have included waivers of points of order—especially points of order under the Congressional Budget Act of 1974—to protect measures, committee or alternative substitutes, or specific floor amendments. During the 97th–99th Congresses (1981–86), a majority of all open rules included at least one waiver: 45.8 percent of the open rules adopted during the 97th Congress were free of waivers, compared with only 29.1 percent during the 98th and 37.7 percent during the 99th. And in each of these three Congresses, between 37.5 and 40.5 percent of all open rules waived enforcement of at least one section of the Budget Act. While budget waivers have not quite become routine, they have become common

26. On June 9, 1988, Democrat Barney Frank of Massachusetts responded to Republican criticisms of restrictive rules by asserting that the Republican leader, Robert Michel of

enough to undermine any expectation that the House will abide by its budget-related rules when there are persuasive policy or political reasons to waive them.

At the same time, the increasing frustrations and delays caused by persistently high budget deficits, and partisan disagreements over how to control them, have made Budget Act waivers a more contentious issue. Consequently, these waivers evidently provoked minority party opposition to special rules that Republicans normally would be expected to support. Including a Budget Act waiver in an open rule has made it three times as likely that a majority of Republicans would oppose it. During the three most recent Congresses, a majority of Republicans voted against only 5.6 percent of the open rules that included no Budget Act waivers, compared with 17.7 percent of the open rules that did waive at least one section of the act.[27] To some degree, therefore, Republican reactions to special rules appear to have been shaped by the waivers they have included as well as by the ways in which they have restricted floor amendments.

Republican votes on individual rules undoubtedly are influenced as well by a complex mix of other factors, including the nature of the legislation, the posture of committee Republicans, the position and persuasiveness of the minority floor manager of the rule, the prospects for Senate action, and the general tenor of party relations in the House. And these relations have become so contentious at times that one might well have expected to find some increase in partisan voting on special rules even if there had been no changes in the character of the rules themselves.[28] To some extent, then, the growing minority party opposition to

Illinois, had supported (or failed to oppose) many of them. *Congressional Record*, daily edition (June 9, 1988), pp. H4106–07. On July 7, Trent Lott replied for the Republicans, arguing that a majority of all House Republicans voting and a majority of elected Republican leaders had opposed 64 percent of the restrictive rules on which the House had voted during the 100th Congress to date. According to Lott, "Republicans can be cooperative and accommodating on truly managerial restrictive rules provided they are treated fairly in the process. . . . And it is the increasing reliance on such rules on controversial bills for the purpose of securing partisan advantage or political cover that is being objected to." *Congressional Record*, daily edition (July 7, 1988), p. H5352.

27. These figures exclude waivers to protect consideration of Senate companion measures, conference reports, or Senate amendments, and waivers included in special rules reported for the sole or primary purpose of protecting general appropriations measures against points of order. The data are for votes on ordering the previous question and on adoption. If there were roll call votes on both, the figures reflect the vote on which there was greater Republican opposition.

28. See David Rapp, "Parties Close Ranks When Control Is At Stake: Partisanship Higher in House than Senate," *Congressional Quarterly Weekly Report*, vol. 46 (January 16, 1988), pp. 101–06.

special rules, whether open, restrictive, or closed, almost certainly has been due to a spillover from other developments in the House, reflecting a more generalized dissatisfaction and even anger with what Republicans have characterized as the partisan procedural maneuvers of the majority party Democrats.

Many of the new generation of GOP members have been more impatient and aggressive than their senior colleagues. The most visible Republican protests often have been led by a group of relatively junior conservative Republicans who organized themselves as the Conservative Opportunity Society (COS) in 1983 during the first session of the 98th Congress.[29] Among their other goals, COS members sought to better focus conservative efforts inside and outside the House. Their best-known activity, the exploitation of one-minute and special-order speeches to chastise the Democrats, produced the "television wars" of 1984.[30] Less well known to the public has been the effort of COS members, such as Robert Walker of Pennsylvania, to pursue legislative guerrilla tactics, by such means as questioning and sometimes objecting to routine unanimous consent requests and even attempting to revive the all but forgotten Calendar Wednesday procedure. They also demanded more record votes, both to slow down floor proceedings and to create a public record that, they apparently hoped, some Democrats would have trouble defending in their reelection campaigns. And in the case of special rules, COS members and other Republican sympathizers became increasingly vocal in their opposition to Democratic procedural innovations.

Indeed, in the 98th and 99th Congresses (1983–86), Walker demanded more roll calls on special rules than anyone else except James Quillen, the ranking Republican on the Rules Committee. Walker and many other Republicans have even broken ranks with Quillen since 1983 to lead the opposition to a number of rules, especially to those, open or otherwise, that waived provisions of the Budget Act to protect committee proposals or Democratic floor amendments. And on more than a dozen occasions between 1983 and 1986, Walker's position attracted the support of the vast majority of House Republicans, sometimes even against the preferences of the Republicans on Rules and the Reagan administration.[31]

29. See Diane Granat, "Televised Partisan Skirmishes Erupt in House," *Congressional Quarterly Weekly Report*, vol. 42 (February 11, 1984), pp. 246–49.

30. One result is that now, during special-order speeches, television cameras sometimes show the entire—usually empty—chamber, not just the members who are speaking.

31. Special rules stimulating disagreement during the 99th Congress between COS members and Republican members of Rules included H. Res. 250, H. Res. 262, H. Res. 266, H. Res. 360, H. Res. 391, H. Res. 450, and H. Res. 472.

The increased levels of Republican opposition to rules, even open rules, also seem to have been a by-product of the House's intensely partisan debates on legislation, as well as incidents—such as the election contest involving Democrat Frank McCloskey of Indiana—that elevated the political temperature on the House floor and increased Republican distrust of Democratic motives and intentions. In reaction, Republican floor activists have found their party colleagues more responsive to their appeals for symbolic votes against rules and more willing to oppose the Democratic position on procedural votes almost as a matter of course. And Republicans generally have been free to oppose rules without worrying about the legislative consequences, because their opposition usually has been unsuccessful.

A Parting Example

The transformation in the provisions of special rules has been accompanied by changing attitudes and expectations and by increasing partisanship. Both Rules Committee members and others now expect special rules that limit and structure amending activity for most controversial measures that reach the floor. While these rules sometimes enjoy bipartisan support, Republicans have become increasingly resentful as Democrats have become increasingly bold in shaping special rules. And, just as the Democrats who appealed to their leaders in 1979 had hoped, the effect has been to limit the uncertainties and political dangers of floor action for the majority party.

The difference in the attitudes of most Democrats and most Republicans toward restrictive rules results in a prickly relationship between the parties. Even when the Rules Committee proposes restrictions on amendments that seemingly accommodate Republican interests, the minority remains sensitive to any innovations in special rules that could come back to haunt them in the future. Take, for example, GOP opposition in May 1988 to H. Res. 457, the rule for considering a foreign aid appropriations bill. This was the first such bill to reach the House floor as a freestanding measure since 1981, largely due to foreign aid's highly controversial nature. During a period of budget stringency, spending for foreign aid is even less popular on the Hill than usual, so wrapping aid appropriations into a last-minute continuing resolution saved time, energy, and political trouble, just as it probably saved the funding levels of the aid programs themselves. In 1988, however, Appropriations Committee Democrats and Republicans managed to come to terms with the Reagan administration on compromise legislation. All parties to the agreement hoped that it would hold together, but they feared that the bill would not survive a barrage of unfriendly floor amendments, particularly from conservative Republicans. So the Rules Committee reported, and the White House supported, a special rule limiting amendments to those that members had submitted to the Rules Committee.[32] But the committee's primary purpose evidently was to protect against surprises; all amendments meeting the advance notification requirement were protected by the rule.

Rules Republican Delbert Latta of Ohio and his partisan colleague, Robert Walker of Pennsylvania, led the charge against the rule. Both objected to imposing such restrictions, even accommodating restrictions, on amendments to a general appropriations bill. There often had been restrictive and closed rules for continuing and supplemental appropriations measures, but not for one of the thirteen regular appropriations bills. Although these bills often received rules, the resolutions usually were designed only to protect provisions of the bills against points of order. In a few unusual cases, the Rules Committee also had proposed limits on amendments touching particularly sensitive political nerves, such as abortion or congressional pay raises. But members could not recall a rule like this one, one that controlled all amendments to a regular appropriations bill.

Republican opponents expressed less concern about what was happening today than about what they feared would happen tomorrow. Walker complained that "once you get a precedent like this we tend to see it come in ways which will not have bipartisan agreement," and Latta predicted that "a succession of these type rules is going to be seen in the future." Latta also argued that although this rule made room for all the amendments that members had said they wanted to offer, "members would still be losing the opportunity to come up with amendments on the floor while the bill is being debated," thereby limiting their ability to adjust their amendments and amending strategy to circumstances as they developed on the floor.[33]

The manager of the rule, Butler Derrick, expressed perplexity at the Republican criticisms. The Rules Committee had been quite generous: "We made every amendment in order that was offered. . . . I do not see what the problem is."[34] But David Obey of Wisconsin, the manager of the appropriations bill, went further, criticizing the Republican argu-

---

32. See John Felton, "House Passes Foreign Aid Spending Measure," *Congressional Quarterly Weekly Report*, vol. 46 (May 28, 1988), pp. 1461–62; and *Congressional Record*, daily edition (May 25, 1988), pp. H3600–03.

33. *Congressional Record*, daily edition (May 25, 1988), pp. H3601–02.

34. Ibid., p. H3602.

ments and contending that the restrictive rule made for more responsible deliberations:

> The only thing that this rule does is to say to each Member of the House that, if they are interested enough to offer an amendment to this bill, they should have enough courtesy toward their colleagues so that it is offered ahead of time, so that individual members who have to vote on it can have the time to analyze it, can have the time to read it, and have the time to understand it. So that they do not have to walk through one of these doors and ask, "What is this thing?", and we say, "We do not know; it was just offered; we do not have the foggiest idea what it really does because nobody has any notice of it."[35]

Obey's response reflected the now familiar priority the majority party often gives to minimizing the uncertainty of floor proceedings, while the Republicans' stance reflected their frequent objections to the incremental but seemingly inexorable spread of restrictive provisions that limit their flexibility on the floor. What gave this debate its unusual twist was the Reagan administration's support for the rule, evidently arising from a fear of amendments by its conservative Republican friends. When the vote came, the rule was adopted easily, with all the participating Democrats voting for it. But there was not much evidence of White House influence, as 144 of 163 Republicans voted "nay" to protest yet one more extension of restrictive provisions in special rules.[36]

The strategic context of floor activity has been altered fundamentally by the shift to more restrictive rules. The possibility of protective rules has become a part of nearly everyone's calculations at early stages in the legislative process for highly controversial measures. Members have educated themselves about the repertoire of restrictive and structuring provisions available to the Rules Committee and are now requesting them on a regular basis. For their part, Rules Committee Democrats recognize that highly restrictive rules are likely to produce significant Republican opposition, so they must look to fellow Democrats for support. Obtaining this support, however, may require concessions to Democrats at the expense of Republicans, reinforcing the partisan pattern of voting on restrictive rules. And for all House members, the time between the end of

35. Ibid., p. H3603.
36. On the other hand, it seems likely that White House urgings were one reason why a number of members failed to offer their amendments that were protected under the rule.

committee markup and the beginning of floor debate has become more important than ever before. What happens during this time —during the "off-stage" negotiations and the Rules Committee's formal meetings that follow—can have as much effect on the final shape of legislation as anything that has happened already or will happen thereafter.

CHAPTER FIVE

Implications and Continuations

IT WOULD BE a mistake to infer from the trends reported in the previous two chapters that the sole or even primary effect of restrictive rules has been to centralize power in the House. The conclusion is tempting. After all, special rules are written by a handful of Rules Committee Democrats, often under the personal direction of the Speaker. Yet there is much more to the story. Restrictive rules serve to reduce the uncertainty of floor decisionmaking not only for Democratic party leaders and Rules Committee members, but also for the standing committees whose legislation is at risk on the floor. To the extent that special rules now shield committee recommendations from certain floor amendments, points of order, and other unfriendly actions, they can reinforce the *decentralized* character of House policymaking. By itself, therefore, the changing pattern of special rules over the last decade does not reveal much about the distribution of power within the House, except, perhaps, that the majority party has asserted itself over the minority party on floor procedure and that the opportunities for rank-and-file members to offer their own amendments on the floor have been limited by restrictive provisions.

This chapter appraises the meaning of the shift to restrictive rules for both the standing committees and the Speaker and for their linkages with the Rules Committee. We first consider the differences in special rules received by the various standing committees of the House, which yield important qualifications about the trends in special rules. We then review the evolving relationship between the Speaker and the Rules Committee during the past two decades. In doing so, we add some perspective to the conclusions of the previous chapters and extend our examination of special rules through the first session of the 100th Congress, under the new Speaker, Jim Wright. We close by highlighting several recent resolutions that illustrate the continuing possibilities and limits of restrictive rules as tools for manipulating policy outcomes on the floor.

Standing Committees and Special Rules

The movement toward restrictive rules has substantially reduced the uncertainties and dangers that legislation can confront on the House floor, to the advantage of the standing committees as well as the majority party's leaders. The surge in amending activity during the 1970s put most committees' bills at greater risk on the floor. More amendments were more likely to be adopted, for the reasons discussed in chapter 2, and such a prospect was even more likely when inexperienced bill managers could not adequately anticipate developments on the floor. Restrictive rules have helped, whether they merely imposed an advance notice requirement on amendments or, at the other extreme, prohibited all unfriendly amendments except a Republican substitute that Democratic party and committee leaders could mobilize to beat. A variety of more recent innovative provisions have served committees in other ways. Alternative substitutes have permitted and even promoted solidarity on the floor among committees sharing jurisdiction over a bill. By using this device or by including self-executing provisions for adopting committee-supported amendments, the Rules Committee can save committees time and inconvenience in some cases and protect them against difficult floor votes in others. And when it is unrealistic to avoid such votes altogether, "king-of-the-mountain" provisions at least can ensure that the choices are arranged to the committee's advantage.

Nevertheless, there are several reasons why the experiences of the House's standing committees with special rules have varied widely. In the first place, committees' legislative agendas differ in size, complexity, and controversy.[1] Consequently, committees also differ in the frequency with which they request special rules and in their interest in receiving protection against floor amendments. For instance, each year the Science, Space, and Technology Committee reports a series of reauthorization bills, each of which requires a rule; but rarely are any of these measures time-consuming or controversial enough to justify restricting the amending process. The Armed Services Committee, on the other hand, comes to the floor less often; but its annual defense authorization bill recently has become such a magnet for amendments that it has received some of

1. See Steven S. Smith and Christopher J. Deering, *Committees in Congress* (Washington, D.C.: CQ Press, 1984), pp. 59–82; Richard F. Fenno, Jr., *Congressmen in Committees* (Little, Brown, 1973), pp. 15–45; and David E. Price, "Policy Making in Congressional Committees: The Impact of 'Environmental' Factors," *American Political Science Review*, vol. 72 (June 1978), pp. 548–74.

the most elaborate and carefully calibrated rules the Rules Committee has devised.

Committees also differ in the opportunities and benefits they offer their members, and other members of the House, in both policy and political terms. Past research on members' reasons for seeking particular committee assignments indicates that three types of motivations predominate. The Committees on Appropriations, Budget, Rules, and Ways and Means are particularly attractive because of the power and prestige they bring their members—by virtue of their jurisdiction over taxing and spending or, in the case of Rules, over every other committee's bills—and because of the breadth of issues that come before them. The rich policy jurisdictions of six other committees, such as Energy and Commerce and Education and Labor, are especially appealing to members with strong policy interests. And yet others—Agriculture and Interior, for example—tend to draw members primarily because of their jurisdictions over matters of keen constituency interest. Of course, the rosters of all committees include members with a complex mix of interests and motivations, but the distinctions among prestige, policy, and constituency committees have proven useful in distinguishing among the predominant tendencies of committees and perspectives of their members.[2]

These jurisdictional and motivational differences are related to each other in ways that produce differences in demands for floor amending opportunities and for insulation from floor amendments. Prestige and policy committees are most likely to report controversial, salient legislation, including the bills that define the most significant differences between the parties. Naturally, therefore, major bills reported by these committees are unlikely to attract the two-thirds majorities needed to pass them under suspension of the rules, so their leaders must request special rules instead. And for the same reasons, their bills are the ones most likely to provoke an extended and unpredictable amending process in Committee of the Whole, creating precisely the kinds of uncertainties and dangers that restrictive rules are so well suited to manage. When tax bills from the Ways and Means Committee were privileged, Wilbur Mills and his predecessors would come to the Rules Committee anyway in search of closed rules. And today, the chairman of the Budget Committee can call up budget resolutions and reconciliation bills to be debated and amended in Committee of the Whole without the need for special rules, but he

---

2. See Charles S. Bullock III, "Motivations for U.S. Congressional Committee Preferences: Freshmen of the 92nd Congress," *Legislative Studies Quarterly*, vol. 1 (May 1976), pp. 201–12; Fenno, *Congressmen in Committees*, pp. 1–14; and Smith and Deering, *Committees in Congress*, pp. 83–124.

seeks them anyway for the benefit of a more limited and structured amendment process.

Constituency-oriented committees, on the other hand, report many measures that leaders and members of both parties consider less vital to collective partisan and national interests. In marking up their bills, these committees also are more likely to have taken account, often through logrolling, of the constituency interests of the members most concerned about them. In fact, representatives with the strongest continuing interest in the work of these committees either hold seats on them or seek assistance of committee members from their state delegations, regional groups, or policy caucuses. And many local-interest amendments that noncommittee members offer to bills such as highway, public works, and water resources measures may be added on the floor without threatening the value of these measures to committee members. In fact, floor managers sometimes accept such amendments willingly in order to attract broader support for their bills. Generally speaking, therefore, the dangers of extended amending marathons in Committee of the Whole are not as severe for constituency-oriented committees, so their need for protective special rules is quite modest in comparison with prestige and policy committees.[3]

Corroborating evidence for this interpretation can be found in table 5-1. The distribution of the Rules Committee's work load is reflected in the number of rules (shown in parentheses) that the House adopted in each Congress for measures reported by each of the standing committees. Much of Rules's work has been generated by the prestigious Committee on Ways and Means, with its jurisdiction over tax, social security, health, and trade matters, and several of the policy-oriented committees—Energy and Commerce, Education and Labor, and Foreign Affairs. Other prestige committees report far fewer measures than Ways and Means, but their legislation almost always generates controversy. In the case of Appropriations, for instance, continuing resolutions and supplemental appropriations bills have been central features of executive-legislative conflict during the last decade.[4] Similarly, the Budget Committee's budget resolutions and reconciliation bills have been at the heart of much of the political debate between the parties and between Congress and the president in the 1980s.

3. On floor amending activity for House committees, see Steven S. Smith, *Call to Order: Floor Politics in the House and Senate* (Brookings, forthcoming), chap. 6.

4. We again exclude regular appropriations bills from our analysis; as privileged measures, these bills either go directly to the floor without special rules, or they receive rules that usually just waive points of order.

TABLE 5-1. Proportions of Restrictive or Closed Rules for Measures
Reported by House Committees, 94th–99th Congresses (1975–86)[a]
Percent

Type of committee	Congress					
	94th ('75–'76)	95th ('77–'78)	96th ('79–'80)	97th ('81–'82)	98th ('83–'84)	99th ('85–'86)
Prestige committees[b]	**65.5**	**82.8**	**84.9**	**94.7**	**89.2**	**89.3**
Appropriations	25.0	60.0	88.2	100.0	85.7	77.8
	(4)	(5)	(17)	(5)	(7)	(9)
Budget	. . .[c]	. . .[c]	100.0	100.0	100.0	100.0
	(0)	(0)	(4)	(4)	(3)	(4)
Rules	80.0	80.0	75.0	75.0	66.7	66.7
	(5)	(5)	(4)	(4)	(3)	(3)
Ways and Means	70.0	89.5	82.1	100.0	91.7	100.0
	(20)	(19)	(28)	(6)	(24)	(12)
Policy committees[b]	**6.7**	**6.9**	**14.8**	**17.9**	**25.4**	**45.6**
Banking, Finance, and	5.6	7.1	0	16.7	0	44.4
Urban Affairs	(18)	(14)	(13)	(6)	(5)	(9)
Foreign Affairs	0	0	7.1	14.3	66.7	69.2
	(24)	(16)	(14)	(7)	(9)	(13)
Energy and Commerce	7.9	8.7	26.7	14.3	31.8	30.8
	(38)	(23)	(30)	(14)	(22)	(13)
Judiciary	17.6	13.3	0	33.3	25.0	66.7
	(17)	(15)	(14)	(9)	(8)	(6)
Education and Labor	0	7.1	28.6	0	5.9	28.6
	(16)	(14)	(7)	(3)	(17)	(14)
Government	16.7	0	33.3	. . .[c]	0	50.0
Operations	(6)	(5)	(3)	(0)	(2)	(2)

As expected, prestige committees have been more likely to receive
restrictive or closed rules than policy committees, and policy committees
more than constituency committees. Even as early as the 94th Congress
(1975–76), when restrictive rules were far less common than they have
since become, only one-third of the rules for prestige committee bills
were fully open rules. Ways and Means, we have already noted, has long
received restrictive and closed rules for tax legislation and other bills.
Table 5-1 indicates that Ways and Means led the way in both the number
and proportion of restrictive rules in the 1970s and continued to do so in
the 1980s. During the 97th–99th Congresses (1981–86), for example,
thirty-nine of the forty-two rules adopted for Ways and Means bills were
either restrictive or closed. The Budget Committee also has received restrictive rules for every one of its budget resolutions and reconciliation
bills, and most continuing resolutions have been partially or wholly closed
to floor amendments.

In the aggregate, policy committees were far less likely than prestige

TABLE 5-1 (*continued*)

	Congress					
Type of committee	94th ('75–'76)	95th ('77–'78)	96th ('79–'80)	97th ('81–'82)	98th ('83–'84)	99th ('85–'86)
Constituency committees[b]	4.2	7.5	9.8	10.4	12.1	43.1
Agriculture	0	0	12.5	25.0	30.0	50.0
	(16)	(8)	(16)	(8)	(10)	(10)
Armed Services	0	0	0	0	16.7	57.1
	(9)	(13)	(10)	(9)	(6)	(7)
Interior and Insular	6.3	4.8	22.2	20.0	0	45.5
Affairs	(16)	(21)	(9)	(10)	(9)	(11)
Merchant Marine and	0	9.1	11.1	0	0	33.3
Fisheries	(5)	(11)	(9)	(3)	(11)	(9)
Public Works and	18.1	33.3	12.5	9.1	12.5	62.5
Transportation	(11)	(9)	(8)	(11)	(8)	(8)
Science, Space, and	0	5.9	0	0	0	0
Technology	(14)	(17)	(8)	(6)	(11)	(6)
Small Business	. . .[c]	0	0	0	50.0	. . .[c]
	(0)	(1)	(1)	(1)	(2)	(0)
Veterans' Affairs	. . .[c]	. . .[c]	. . .[c]	. . .[c]	100.0	. . .[c]
	(0)	(0)	(0)	(0)	(1)	(0)
Other committees						
District of Columbia	. . .[c]	. . .[c]	0	. . .[c]	. . .[c]	. . .[c]
	(0)	(0)	(2)	(0)	(0)	(0)
House Administration	42.9	33.3	100.0	0	100.0	0
	(7)	(3)	(1)	(1)	(1)	(1)
Post Office and Civil	0	10.0	0	100.0	100.0	33.3
Service	(17)	(10)	(4)	(1)	(1)	(3)

a. Each cell entry is the proportion of all the special rules adopted for initial consideration of measures reported from a committee during a Congress. Numbers in parentheses are the total number of all rules for each committee. Multiple-committee measures are counted for each committee involved, and multiple rules for the same measure are included. Rules providing solely or primarily for waivers of points of order, as for most appropriations bills, are excluded. The Committee on Standards of Official Conduct has been excluded.

b. The entries for the three major committee types are the aggregate proportions for the committees in each category.

c. No rules were adopted during this Congress for initial floor consideration of measures reported by this committee.

committees to receive restrictive rules during the six Congresses shown here. During the 94th and 95th Congresses, no policy committee brought more than a total of five measures to the floor under special rules with restrictive provisions. But the aggregate trend line for these committees is equally noteworthy. Restrictive and closed rules became increasingly common after 1979, when the Democratic leadership began to look more frequently to provisions limiting floor amendments in order to structure and control floor deliberations.[5] The frequency of such rules for policy

5. With such small numbers of rules, unique cases can create distortions and misleading impressions. During the 99th Congress, for example, the Rules Committee reported three

committee measures more than doubled between the 94th–95th Congresses (1975–78) and the 96th–97th Congresses (1979–82), and was more than six times higher during the 99th Congress than it had been during the 94th. Several committees that had little hope of obtaining restrictive or closed rules in the 1970s found that some of their bills were encountering waves of floor amendments, so they have begun to request and receive restrictive rules more often in recent Congresses. The Judiciary Committee's bill to revise the federal rules of criminal procedure and the Simpson-Mazzoli immigration bills were cases in point, as was the nuclear freeze resolution reported by the Foreign Affairs Committee.

By the 99th Congress, nearly all the House's standing committees had some experience with restrictive rules, either for their own bills or for bills over which they shared jurisdiction. And the taste for these rules, once acquired, can be addictive. Consequently, as noted in chapter 3, Rules Committee members now sometimes find themselves in the awkward position of having to fend off what they consider to be frivolous requests for protective provisions in special rules, as committee and subcommittee leaders seek to take advantage of the Rules Committee's procedural arsenal. To a considerable degree, therefore, the strategic calculations of House committee leaders have been altered fundamentally by the shift to restrictive rules.

The magnitude of the trend toward rules limiting floor amendments, however important it may be, must not be exaggerated. Restrictive and closed rules are still the exception for all but the four prestige committees. Most House committees continue to bring most of their major legislation—those measures receiving a special rule—to the floor under open rules. Even the most active policy committee, Energy and Commerce, received restrictive rules for less than a third of its measures in the 98th and 99th Congresses; and among the policy and constituency committees, only Foreign Affairs received restrictive or closed rules more than half the time during the same four-year period. Nonetheless, the demand for restrictive rules certainly has become more widespread. Although we lack systematic data on instances in which the Rules Committee has rejected requests for restrictive rules, Rules rarely has reported them without having been asked to do so by the committees of jurisdiction. Clearly, then, the House's committees perceive a continuing threat from floor amendments. And while the Rules Committee continues to discriminate in reporting restrictive rules, it has become more willing to

different restrictive rules, only one of which was adopted, for considering the massive antidrug bill of 1986, which was the product of a dozen House committees. This yielded committee and aggregate data that are somewhat inflated.

do so for more committees, especially during the 99th Congress. In that Congress, the Committee on Science, Space, and Technology was the only one of the prestige, policy, and constituency committees that brought measures to the floor under special rules and failed to receive at least one restrictive or closed rule.[6] The other committees received such rules between 28 and 100 percent of the time. In short, restrictive rules have become an option that more of the House's standing committees now consider more often.

Unquestionably, therefore, the House's committees and its committee system have benefited from the transformation of special rules from rather simple devices for getting measures to the floor to more sophisticated tactical weapons. The magnitude of the benefit is difficult to gauge in policy terms, of course, but committees' appeals for restrictive rules, and the Rules Committee's willingness to grant them, are the best evidence of their perceived value. They have protected individual committee and subcommittee chairmen, and ultimately the House as a whole, from some of the consequences of the reforms of the 1970s, as the legacy of these changes affected both the powers and expertise of committees and members' attitudes toward them. Moreover, the data in table 5-1 actually understate the extent to which the House has come to make its policy decisions under the terms of restrictive rules because of Congress's growing reliance on continuing resolutions, reconciliation bills, and other omnibus measures, which have been used to package legislation that otherwise would have been considered as separate measures under less restrictive special rules.

The Majority Leadership and the Rules Committee

By no means have the House's Democratic party leaders and the Rules Committee sought to carefully orchestrate floor deliberations for all legislation. The House has passed large numbers of measures in recent years under suspension of the rules, which protects them against all floor amendments. In addition, the changing provisions of special rules, on which we have focused most of our attention, should not mask another striking development: a sharp decline in the total number of special rules that the House has adopted for bringing measures to the floor. The number of these resolutions fell by half between the 94th and 98th Congresses, from 248 to 125, and continued to decline during the 99th (see

6. Another exception was the House Administration Committee, but it received only one special rule.

table 3-1). We also showed in chapter 3 that, among the bills and resolutions receiving rules, restrictive rules have been most common for "key vote" measures and those affecting the jurisdictions of multiple committees, and we have observed in this chapter that such rules are most common for the legislation of the top money committees and a few other House committees. Clearly, it is the major, controversial measures—legislation that would likely provoke the most unpredictable floor amending activity—that have stimulated special rules crafted to include restrictions on amendments and other innovative provisions.[7]

Beyond question, though, the new craftsmanship that representatives have witnessed has been the product of a partnership—Republicans might characterize it as an open conspiracy—between the Speaker and his leadership associates and their fellow partisans on the Rules Committee. But few would consider it an equal partnership. Ever since 1975, when the Speaker gained the authority to appoint Rules Committee Democrats with the approval of the Democratic Caucus, they have been expected to serve as an arm of the majority party leadership, arranging the timing and design of special rules in ways that respond to the prevailing interests of the majority party as articulated by the Speaker.[8] This relationship is the foundation upon which the new pattern of special rules has been built. For the 1977 energy package, the Speaker sought and obtained a highly restrictive rule, contrary to the preferences of several Rules Committee Democrats; as we mentioned, this rule later was cited as having encouraged leaders and members alike to start thinking more seriously about the virtues of restricting amendments to non–Ways and Means bills. And in 1979, it was Speaker O'Neill, responding to demands from his rank-and-file members, who gave his approval to the preference of Richard Bolling and Gillis Long to be more aggressive in designing restrictive rules. Yet the relationship between the Speaker and Rules

7. In fact, these developments suggest a bifurcation of sorts in the House's legislative floor agenda between the bulk of bills and resolutions, which are so noncontroversial they can be passed by unanimous consent or by two-thirds votes under suspension, and the much smaller number of far more controversial bills, which are accompanied by restrictive rules. The decline appears to have come among bills of moderate importance considered under open rules.

8. See Bruce I. Oppenheimer, "The Rules Committee: New Arm of Leadership in a Decentralized House," in Lawrence C. Dodd and Bruce I. Oppenheimer, eds., *Congress Reconsidered* (Praeger, 1977), pp. 96–116; Oppenheimer, "The Changing Relationship Between House Leadership and the Committee on Rules," in Frank H. Mackaman, ed., *Understanding Congressional Leadership* (Washington, D.C.: Congressional Quarterly Press, 1981), pp. 207–25; and Barbara Sinclair, *Majority Leadership in the U.S. House* (Johns Hopkins University Press, 1983), pp. 77–85.

Democrats has undergone a few twists and turns that are both reflected in and a reflection of complex special rules.

During the 1970s Speakers Carl Albert and Tip O'Neill continued the practice begun by Sam Rayburn, after the 1961 fight to expand the Rules Committee, to appoint Democrats to Rules only if they were likely to support party positions as each Speaker understood them. Albert took a more active interest in Rules's decisions than his predecessor, John McCormack, and both he and O'Neill endorsed the view that special rules should be written with the majority party's interests in mind. The committee was no longer an obstacle to sending to the floor bills that were important to Democratic leaders. Instead, Bruce Oppenheimer explains, Rules Democrats assisted their leaders in directing traffic on the floor, provided a dress rehearsal in the form of their hearings for committee and subcommittee chairmen, and, to a lesser degree, served as field commanders for the leadership by providing intelligence on potential political and scheduling problems.[9] But above all, the committee's main job, even during the mid-1970s, was simply to report open rules at the request of the majority party leaders. These tasks were important, but not particularly challenging. The Rules Committee no longer was the independent power center it once had been, and its stature in the House suffered.

Under O'Neill, who replaced Albert in 1977, the ties between the Speaker and the committee were protected and strengthened by Richard Bolling. His close working relationship with the new Speaker, cultivated since 1955 when O'Neill became a member of Rules, and his commitment to the principle of strong party leadership made Bolling a natural liaison between Rules and the Speaker's office. Bolling also was more than willing to explain how special rules could and should be used more creatively, and he frequently made suggestions to the Speaker. In addition, he served as the floor manager for a disproportionate number of the relatively few complex rules that were reported during the mid-1970s.[10] After Bolling became Rules Committee chairman in 1979, he acted without explicit guidance from O'Neill on the vast majority of bills that came before Rules, although he consulted frequently with O'Neill's staff. When controversies over floor tactics for major bills threatened to develop among House Democrats, O'Neill and other party leaders played a more

9. Oppenheimer, "The Changing Relationship Between House Leadership and the Committee on Rules," pp. 216–18.

10. Ibid., pp. 221–22. The term "complex" is used here in a more general sense than in chapter 3. Oppenheimer described as "complex" virtually any rule that was neither open nor closed, including the few rules that explicitly restricted amending activity.

direct role, but even then Bolling was considered an integral part of the leadership team.[11]

O'Neill's reliance on Bolling, as well as on his own top aide, Ari Weiss, meant that there were only a very few "artisans" who were actively engaged in crafting special rules, and this was an arrangement that suited O'Neill very well. Except when partisan or factional needs required his personal intervention, O'Neill preferred not to be troubled with the minutiae of writing rules. Bolling could enjoy his central role while at the same time serving as a buffer between O'Neill and other members of both parties when they had complaints about special rules. Some of his fellow Democrats on Rules resented Bolling's occasional heavy-handedness and sometimes wondered if the chairman was speaking for the Speaker or for himself. But few could doubt that the informal working relationship between O'Neill and Bolling had increased the importance of special rules and restored some of the discretion and influence the Rules Committee had lost in the early 1970s.

When Bolling retired in 1982, at the end of the 97th Congress, the chairmanship was assumed by Claude Pepper, who was not as assertive as Bolling nor as much a master of the intricacies of House procedure. Rules's decisionmaking became a more collegial enterprise, at least among the Democrats. The party leadership still was actively involved on major issues, but, as we noted in chapter 2, Pepper reported that he very seldom received guidance from the Speaker during 1985–86 on the design of special rules. Instead, it was the Rules Democrats, with their expanding repertoire of provisions and options, who were engaged more collectively and independently in devising special rules for the vast majority of bills before the committee.

The proportion of restrictive rules proceeded to climb to record levels during the 99th Congress (1985–86), as we have shown. And very rarely did the committee so misjudge the policy and political situation that its proposals were amended or defeated. The exercise of such power with discretion breeds respect, if not appreciation, from all members of the House. As one Rules Democrat put it in early 1987, "I've been introduced by colleagues to groups or constituents as a respected member of the powerful Rules Committee. I'm not really comfortable with that, but I get the message."[12] However, most of his colleagues relished their situation; at least for the postreform period, the 99th Congress was the apex of Rules Democrats' power.

11. Personal interviews with Richard Bolling, October 24, 1986, and Ari Weiss, July 19, 1987.

12. Anonymous interview with one of the authors.

The relationship between the Speaker and the committee remains very much a matter of personalities and personal relationships, so it was not surprising that it began to change considerably after Jim Wright was elected Speaker in 1987 to replace O'Neill. Adjectives that soon were applied to Wright included aggressive, impatient, temperamental, daring, and partisan, and many of the same adjectives have characterized the relationship he initially established with Rules Democrats.[13] Wright made it clear from the outset that he would be much more actively involved in the committee's work than his predecessor had been, in terms of both the number of bills in which he would take an interest and the design of special rules for considering them. He did not wait for tactical disputes among Democrats to stimulate his involvement; as majority leader, he had learned to think in terms of special rules as he began formulating his legislative strategies, and he did not share O'Neill's willingness to delegate. Anxious to move major Democratic bills swiftly and establish himself as Speaker early in his first term, Wright pushed highway, water projects, trade, and other bills to the floor in rapid succession during the opening months of the 100th Congress. His insistence on keeping legislation moving according to his schedule led him to demand and obtain rules to restrict amending activity, limit floor debates, and reduce some of the risks to his legislative program. Of the first nine rules of the 100th Congress, eight were closed or highly restrictive.

Predictably, the Rules Committee once again found itself at the center of partisan controversy, although much of the Republican criticism of restrictive and closed rules was directed more at the new Speaker than at the committee itself.[14] Some of Wright's colleagues believed that he was

13. On Wright's style, see Steve Blakely, "Speaker Style: Jim Wright and the FSLIC Bill," *Congressional Quarterly Weekly Report*, vol. 45 (May 23, 1987), p. 1110; Jacqueline Calmes, "The Hill Leaders: Their Places on the Ladder," *Congressional Quarterly Weekly Report*, vol. 45 (January 3, 1987), pp. 5–10; Richard E. Cohen, "Quick-Starting Speaker," *National Journal*, vol. 19 (May 30, 1987), pp. 1409–13; Cohen, "Wright Angle," *National Journal*, vol. 19 (October 17, 1987), p. 2633; Cohen, "Full Speed Ahead," *National Journal*, vol. 20 (January 30, 1988), pp. 238–44; Maureen Dowd, "All Eyes on Wright and His Brows," *New York Times*, January 23, 1987, p. A12; Jonathan Fuerbringer, "Speaker of the House Wright Takes His Leadership by the Horns," *New York Times*, April 7, 1987, p. A32; Janet Hook, "House Leadership Elections: Wright Era Begins," *Congressional Quarterly Weekly Report*, vol. 44 (December 13, 1986), pp. 3067–72; Hook, "Speaker Jim Wright Takes Charge in the House," *Congressional Quarterly Weekly Report*, vol. 45 (July 11, 1987), pp. 1483–88; Hook, "Jim Wright: Taking Big Risks to Amass Power," *Congressional Quarterly Weekly Report*, vol. 46 (March 12, 1988), pp. 623–26; and Steven Komarow, "Speaker Wright's First Year: Taking House by the Horns," *Arlington Journal*, December 30, 1987.

14. See Janet Hook, "GOP Chafes Under House Restrictive Rules," *Congressional Quarterly Weekly Report*, vol. 45 (October 10, 1987), pp. 2449–52. Also revealing were the floor

failing to take full advantage of having Rules Democrats so well positioned to serve as "field commanders" and buffers. And some Democrats, even some members of Rules, were reported to be resentful when Wright expected them to approve particular rules with little advance consultation. From the perspective of the Rules Committee, the Speaker's personal involvement in its decisions meant a loss of institutional discretion, which, if continued, would mean a loss of personal power for the committee's members.

On balance, the record of special rules for the entire first session of the 100th Congress (1987) was not very different, at least quantitatively, from the pattern of the two preceding Congresses. Nearly 41 percent of all rules for the session were restrictive or closed, down slightly from the rate of nearly 45 percent for the previous Congress.[15] The forms and extent of restrictions in special rules limiting floor amendments also were consistent with those of the preceding four years. Over three-fifths of the restrictive rules designated the amendments that were in order and one-half of those rules permitted only one or two amendments (compare with tables 3-5 and 3-6). The overall pattern for 1987 reflected the return to more routine business after the first few months of the session. The initial series of restrictive and closed rules that generated so much criticism was followed by a comparable series of conventional open rules, but for much less significant legislation.[16]

The Possibilities and Limitations of Craftsmanship

The process of innovation we discussed toward the end of chapter 3 also continued into the 100th Congress as Speaker Wright and the Rules Committee mixed existing procedures into new combinations and adapted

---

statements made by the Republican members of Rules, especially by Trent Lott, who periodically inserted in the *Record* a running summary of the kinds of rules the committee was reporting. For example, see *Congressional Record*, daily edition (July 22, 1987), p. H6457; (November 20, 1987), p. E4580; (December 22, 1987), p. E4981; and (May 24, 1988), pp. H3578–79.

15. The figures for the first session of the 100th Congress were as follows: 59.3 percent open, 27.1 percent restrictive, and 13.6 percent closed. The comparison with the 99th Congress should not be read as suggesting greater leniency on Speaker Wright's part, because one would expect a higher percentage of rules reported toward the end of the Congress to include restrictive provisions, thereby increasing the overall frequency of restrictive rules for the Congress.

16. It also may have reflected the beginning of a movement toward more latitude in the relationship between Speaker Wright and the Rules Democrats. See Cohen, "Wright Angle," p. 2633.

them to suit other circumstances. The special rules the House adopted in 1987 for three measures demonstrate both the possibilities and limitations of using restrictive rules to respond to difficult institutional and political problems.

The extent to which the Rules Committee and the House are now prepared to use special rules to fine-tune the amending process was demonstrated by the three rules members approved for considering a single measure, H.R. 1748, the defense authorization bill for fiscal year 1988.[17] The first of the three effectively gave members the chance to vote on which version of the bill they wanted to continue debating and amending. The second and third rules proceeded to designate precisely which amendments members could then offer, but these rules hardly were very restrictive, as they permitted consideration of more than 125 different amendments. In this respect, these rules clearly were designed to define the outer bounds of the amending process, not to limit it in any significant way. But probably of greater importance was the order in which certain amendments could be proposed.

Under the terms of these rules, votes on some of the vital amendments the Reagan administration opposed were dispersed among votes on less crucial amendments supported by the administration. In this way, moderate and conservative Democrats, whose votes the majority leadership needed on its key amendments, had opportunities to demonstrate support for Reagan administration positions yet were still able to vote for their party's positions on the few most significant amendments. The rules also adapted to new circumstances "king-of-the-mountain" procedures (under which the last of several competing alternatives to win majority support is the one that finally prevails). These procedures had been reserved for choosing among alternative versions of bills, but now they were applied to pairs or groups of amendments on six different subjects, all contained within the same defense bill. For example, four amendments relating to the strategic defense initiative were arranged so that members could vote for the proposal favored by the president, but could then also vote for the one sponsored by Charles Bennett of Florida, which the Democratic leadership preferred. Majority votes for both would mean a victory for the Bennett amendment. In fact, twenty-one members did vote for both amendments, although the administration proposal lost by six votes and the Bennett amendment was adopted by a twenty-vote mar-

17. H. Res. 152, adopted on April 30, 1987; H. Res. 156, adopted on May 6, 1987; and H. Res. 160, adopted on May 7, 1987.

gin.[18] For this bill, some observers noted, structuring the amending process was as important as restricting it.[19]

If these rules illustrate the extreme limits of complexity and intricacy that special rules have attained, attempts to incorporate a major welfare reform proposal in the 1987 reconciliation bill demonstrate that there still are limits to the House's tolerance for restrictive rules.[20] The welfare reform package included components developed by four committees and was consolidated by the Rules Committee as it prepared to report a rule for the reconciliation bill. The rule, H. Res. 296, proposed to incorporate the 148-page welfare reform proposal into the bill by means of a self-executing provision, which stated that, upon adoption of the rule, the package would be considered as having been adopted in Committee of the Whole and in the House.[21] The only floor amendment in order was to be a set of amendments, including the Republican amendments to the welfare proposal, to be offered en bloc by Minority Leader Robert Michel. The only way to oppose the Democratic welfare plan would be to support the Republican plan instead.

Although self-executing provisions had been used previously, the welfare reform package was easily the most important legislation yet treated in this way. As discussed in chapter 3, most such provisions had been designed to cure technical or procedural problems, so they had not been particularly controversial. But in reporting H. Res. 296, the Rules Committee and the Speaker had adapted the device to protect a controversial proposal from a direct floor vote. Not surprisingly, Trent Lott objected on behalf of the Republicans:

> This is what is called a self-executing rule. Back in the old days, the Rules Committee only used this procedure for making technical

18. Pat Towell, "House Slashes President's SDI Request in Move to Slow Push for Deployment," *Congressional Quarterly Weekly Report*, vol. 45 (May 16, 1987), pp. 974–75.

19. See Pat Towell, "House Rebuffs Reagan Views on Defense Spending, Policy," *Congressional Quarterly Weekly Report*, vol. 45 (May 9, 1987), pp. 900–03.

20. See Janet Hook, "Bitterness Lingers From House Budget Votes," *Congressional Quarterly Weekly Report*, vol. 45 (November 7, 1987), pp. 2712–13; Patrick L. Knudsen, "House Will Try Again on Welfare Overhaul," *Congressional Quarterly Weekly Report*, vol. 45 (October 31, 1987), p. 2655; Spencer Rich, "House Leaders Clear Way for Cut in Welfare Bill," *Washington Post*, December 11, 1987, p. A4; Rich, "Welfare-Overhaul Bill Passes Big Test," *Washington Post*, December 16, 1987, p. A10; and Elizabeth Wehr, "Wright Finds a Vote to Pass Reconciliation Bill," *Congressional Quarterly Weekly Report*, vol. 45 (October 31, 1987), pp. 2653–55.

21. If the rule had not provided for the welfare amendment to be considered as having been adopted in the House as well as in Committee of the Whole, there could have been a separate vote on it after the Committee of the Whole rose and reported the bill back to the House with the amendments it had adopted.

or minor and noncontroversial amendments to a bill. But, this procedure is being used more and more lately for the automatic adoption of substantive and controversial provisions.

Let's briefly go down the list of self-executing amendments that you will be adopting by voting for this rule. The first three strike provisions which were objected to by other committees: the ethanol fuel provision, the cotton promotion fees, and the coal tariff. Those I have no problem with.

But, the next three amendments strike all the Education and Labor and Ways and Means welfare provisions, and then insert a whole new, 148-page welfare reform compromise which no one on the Rules Committee had seen when we reported this rule, which no one could explain, and which no one could provide a cost estimate.[22]

The "old days" extended back only several years. But during that short time, an innovation in special rules had become so well accepted that using it for more partisan and controversial purposes could provoke protests that this resolution would violate established practice. But if Republican leaders were surprised and disappointed by the rule, Democratic leaders were even more surprised and disappointed when forty-eight Democrats, mostly conservatives who disapproved of the welfare reform package as part of a deficit reduction bill, voted with the Republicans to defeat the rule. The Speaker and the committee had miscalculated. As Dan Glickman, Democrat of Kansas, said, "When there is grumbling from the membership, it needs to be listened to. The antennae need to be out a little higher."[23]

While the Democratic leadership quickly arranged for a new rule on the reconciliation bill, welfare reform was dropped. Instead, its supporters planned to bring the welfare package to the floor several weeks later as a separate bill. The rule proposed for the bill provided only for one Republican substitute until seventy-nine Democrats wrote to the Speaker to protest the fact that other substitutes would not be in order. After rechecking his vote count, Wright asked the Rules Committee to write a new rule. This second resolution, H. Res. 298, permitted one additional amendment sponsored by Michael Andrews, Democrat of Texas, which offered a compromise by reducing the costs of the Democratic plan, but not to the levels of the Republican alternative. The House agreed to

22. *Congressional Record*, daily edition (October 29, 1987), p. H9131.
23. Quoted in Hook, "Bitterness Lingers From House Budget Votes," p. 2717.

these new procedural ground rules, adopting H. Res. 298 by a 213–206 vote, as Democratic leaders managed to gain the support of twenty-two Democrats who had voted against the original reconciliation rule. The Andrews amendment was adopted.

As this episode demonstrates, there are persistent limits on leadership in the House and on the Rules Committee's discretion in designing special rules. On politically sensitive issues, members' support for special rules is entwined with their policy preferences. Majority party leaders may still find it somewhat easier to convince some of their colleagues to support them on what are ostensibly "procedural" votes on rules than on more directly "substantive" votes on amendments and bills. But as the importance and effects of special rules become more widely appreciated, it must be increasingly difficult for members to explain how they can vote for a rule that precludes consideration of a proposal they claim to support. And no matter what the relations between the Democratic Speaker and the Democratic members of Rules, the limits on the committee's discretion are tighter when Republicans are united against its proposals, as they were on the defeated reconciliation rule and as they have been on many other occasions. The Democrats then must assume that they have to create majorities solely from among their own numbers. Confronting a unified Republican opposition, they cannot afford to lose many Democratic votes, whether for philosophical, jurisdictional, or personal reasons. There is very little margin for error.

A final example is the highly restrictive rule crafted in early 1988 for acting on Democratic and Republican proposals for aiding the Nicaraguan contras. Democratic leaders had convinced the House to reject President Reagan's plan, but only by promising a prompt vote on an alternative package they would assemble. This commitment posed a particularly difficult tactical problem for the Democrats who were charged with meeting it. On their left, they faced liberal Democrats who opposed any aid at all; on their right, conservative Democrats and the vast majority of Republicans insisted on a much larger and less restricted aid package than the Democratic leadership could support. Democrat Barney Frank of Massachusetts described the problem: "Our goal is to find something that's 60 percent acceptable to 52 percent of the members and I think we have a 75 percent chance of doing that." [24]

While forging their aid package, Democratic party leaders also considered how they would present it on the floor, especially in light of two

---

24. Quoted in Tom Kenworthy, "Hill Democrats Draft Nonlethal Contra Aid," *Washington Post*, February 24, 1988, p. A1.

factors: first, an understanding with Republican leaders that Republicans could present an alternative to it; and second, concerns that some Democrats would, from choice or necessity, vote for any aid package and that other Democrats would vote against any aid package. The ideal solution to the tactical problem would be a parliamentary situation in which the latter group of Democrats would have to vote for the majority leadership plan in order to protect against an even worse outcome, the success of the Republican alternative. The special rule that the Rules Committee reported, H. Res. 390, sought this ideal by providing for the House to take up a joint resolution consisting of the Republican aid package, to which the Democratic proposal would be offered as an amendment in the nature of a substitute. Thus the first vote would be a choice between the two plans, but it would take the form of a vote on the Democratic version; and if it won, there would be no direct vote on the Republican alternative.[25]

Democratic leaders could think that, under these circumstances, some Democrats who preferred to oppose all aid would be persuaded to vote "aye" on the first vote in support of their leaders' position, because if it failed, Republicans and conservative Democrats might combine to pass the more objectionable alternative. And if a majority voted for the Democratic substitute, Republicans would be presumed to have little choice but to support passage of the joint resolution as amended. Liberals would be faced with a choice between two options and could not afford to oppose both; instead, they would limit the damage by accepting the lesser of the two evils. And if all went according to plan, Republicans and conservative Democrats then would have a choice between a package they considered inadequate or no package at all.

Republicans objected that these arrangements violated their understanding that the House would be given an opportunity to vote on their package. Minority Leader Michel exclaimed, "Seldom in my tenure in Congress has the Democratic majority exercised such abuse of the legislative process as they have in the procedures which have been forced upon us for considering the Speaker's contra-aid proposal."[26] Notwith-

---

25. See *Congressional Record,* daily edition (March 3, 1988), p. H643. The special rule also provided that if the Republicans did not call up their proposal under the rule, the Democrats could bring up their package, to which floor amendments were prohibited. Some accounts gave much of the credit for designing this rule to David Bonior, chief deputy whip and head of his party's task force on contra aid as well as a member of Rules; see, for instance, Tom Kenworthy, "Bonior: Adroit Engineer of Contra Aid Procedure," *Washington Post,* March 3, 1988, p. A10.

26. Quoted in Tom Kenworthy, "GOP Opposes Contra Aid Voting Plan," *Washington Post,* March 2, 1988, p. A4.

standing such complaints, the House adopted H. Res. 390 on a nearly straight party-line vote; but the carefully constructed plan only half worked. The Democratic substitute was adopted, 215–210. On final passage, however, fifteen Democrats who had voted for the amendment voted against the joint resolution, primarily because they opposed all aid to the contras, and the joint resolution was defeated, 208–216, with only five Republicans voting for it. The special rule had given the Democrats an important procedural advantage, but their tactical calculations were predicated on an assumption that Republicans would act "rationally," accepting something in preference to nothing. Republicans claimed victory for having defeated the Democratic plan and embarrassing the Speaker in the process. But it was not the victory that GOP members had sought and might well have won if the sequence of choices had been arranged differently.

In all three cases—defense authorization, welfare reform, and aid to the contras—Rules Democrats and Democratic leaders had shown considerable creativity in crafting special rules. In each case, the rules structured the consideration of floor amendments in an advantageous manner. Normal relations among amendments were altered in the first two cases, and the conventional relationship between a Democratic proposal and a Republican substitute was reversed for the contra aid measure. In the latter two cases, all points of order were waived against the alternative proposals to permit each side to package its proposals as it saw fit. And in all three cases, the minority party was given an opportunity to have its version considered, although in the last case that opportunity was contingent on defeating the Democratic proposal first. Although the possibilities for designing special rules may not be limitless, they clearly are far more diverse than members could have imagined or would have accepted a generation ago. The dichotomous choice between simple open and closed rules is very much a thing of the past.

On the other hand, these three cases also point to the limits of procedural strategy. Although elements of the defense authorization rules were arranged to promote Democratic positions, the three resolutions were largely the products of bipartisan negotiations involving Les Aspin and William Dickinson, the chairman and ranking Republican on the Armed Services Committee. In permitting well over one hundred amendments, the Rules Committee sought primarily to accommodate members' desires in an orderly way, not to impose anything remotely resembling a gag rule. And in the cases of welfare reform and contra aid, procedural craftsmanship could not really succeed in creating and sustaining majorities that simply were not there. So long as the Rules Committee can only propose, not impose, its special rules, parliamentary ingenuity will remain a useful complement to, but a poor substitute for, the ultimate currency of success in the House: votes.

If these cases illustrate procedural creativity and craftsmanship, a final episode from the 100th Congress is a reminder of where authority in the House finally resides. In this instance, the Rules Committee reached too far. It failed to attract the majority of votes it needed, even on a politically popular issue of immense importance to the chairman of the committee. And it failed because, on this rare occasion, its normal alliance with party and committee leaders had crumbled.

At issue was what became known as the "Pepper bill," a long-term home health care bill cosponsored by Claude Pepper, better known to the public as a champion of senior citizens than as chairman of the Rules Committee, and Edward Roybal of California, chairman of the House Select Committee on Aging.[27] Their bill, which they introduced in June 1987, had been referred routinely to the Energy and Commerce and Ways and Means committees, neither of which seemed very likely to recommend its passage. So Pepper announced his intention to ask Rules to allow him to propose the text of his bill as an amendment to H.R. 2470, a related Medicare Catastrophic Protection Act. But this stratagem raised fears that the catastrophic care bill would sink beneath the added weight of Pepper's amendment. At this point, the Speaker entered the negotiations and ultimately persuaded Pepper to leave H.R. 2470 unencumbered in return for the promise that he and Roybal would have their day on the House floor, but not until the House had resolved its differences with the Senate over the final terms of the other health care bill.

Having agreed to this compromise, Pepper and his allies turned their attention to H.R. 3436, an unobtrusive bill reported by the Education and Labor Committee to make technical changes in the Older Americans Act. On November 18, Pepper alerted the House to what the Rules Committee already had done and what remained for it to do:

> Mr. Speaker, I rise to inform the House that the Rules Committee today reported a rule providing for the consideration of H.R. 3436. The rule makes in order the consideration, as original text, of an amendment of mine which would provide long-term home health care to the chronically ill of all ages. The text of my amend-

27. On these events, see Julie Rovner, "'Pepper Bill' Pits Politics Against Process," *Congressional Quarterly Weekly Report*, vol. 46 (June 4, 1988), pp. 1491–93; and Rovner, "Long-Term Care Bill Derailed—For Now," *Congressional Quarterly Weekly Report*, vol. 46 (June 11, 1988), pp. 1604–05.

ment is printed in the report which accompanies the rule. The rule provides that only amendments which will be printed in a supplemental report will be in order during the bill's consideration.

Any member who may wish to offer an amendment to my substitute should submit his or her amendment to the Rules Committee. Members may begin to submit their amendments immediately and the Rules Committee will notify those members when a meeting of the committee is scheduled to consider the supplemental report. The committee will consider for inclusion in the supplemental report all of those amendments which are received by a deadline which will be announced at some later date. We will determine that deadline after the leadership has notified us that the bill has been scheduled for consideration on the floor.[28]

There was nothing particularly subtle about the chairman's plan, nor about the terms of the rule, H. Res. 314, that the Rules Committee had reported. Pepper would bring the text of his bill to the floor, in the form of an amendment in the nature of a substitute for the text of H.R. 3436, even though his actual bill remained in the files of Energy and Commerce and Ways and Means. The Rules Committee would effectively take Pepper's bill from the control of the other two committees, against their will, and his amendment would become the proverbial "tail wagging the dog" of Education and Labor's minor bill.[29] If members wanted to amend Pepper's proposal, they could submit their amendments to Rules, which eventually would issue a supplemental report listing the amendments it proposed to make in order. And H. Res. 314 authorized Rules to file this report "at any time prior to consideration of the bill," so the House could even be asked to vote for or against the rule before knowing precisely what amendments it would permit members to offer to the Pepper bill.

It was not until June 2, 1988, that the House finally approved the conference report on H.R. 2470, setting the stage for the expected floor fight over Pepper's rule and the amendment it would bring to the House floor. Dan Rostenkowski, chairman of Ways and Means, already had publicly criticized Pepper's plan as an unjustifiable intrusion into his committee's authority and jurisdiction. In a public letter addressed to his "Dear Colleague," Rostenkowski had written on May 23 that "the committee of

28. *Congressional Record*, daily edition (November 18, 1987), p. H10548.
29. During the later floor debate, Pepper asserted that Education and Labor had reported H.R. 3436 "with the clear understanding" that it would become the vehicle for his long-term health care amendment. *Congressional Record*, daily edition (June 8, 1988), p. H4016.

jurisdiction has been effectively discharged, without the normal requirements and procedures for such action having been followed. . . . I cannot remember a more serious violation of the House rules, and am very concerned about the precedent this will set for all House committees."[30] In turn, Rules had supplanted H. Res. 314 by reporting a new rule, H. Res. 466, that was even more restrictive: it proposed to allow only one amendment to Pepper's proposal, a Republican alternative to be offered by Minority Leader Michel.

When Pepper called up H. Res. 466 on June 8, and push finally came to shove on the House floor, members witnessed an extraordinary scene: an open split among some of the most powerful Democrats in the House, as Rostenkowski was joined in opposing Pepper and the rule by John Dingell, chairman of Energy and Commerce, an equally influential (some would say intimidating) presence on Capitol Hill. Pepper opened the debate by trying to puncture the hopes of members that they could cast a "procedural vote" against the rule without being marked as an opponent of a proposal that seemed to enjoy widespread and intense voter appeal. "A vote against the rule is a vote against the bill," Pepper told his colleagues and the TV cameras, "and a vote against the wish of the American people to have its Congress enact a law which protects them from financial disaster in the face of chronic illness."[31]

Dingell responded by expressing his "great affection" for Pepper and his "personal distress" at having to oppose him. But he proceeded to denounce H. Res. 466 in terms reminiscent of hundreds of Republican speeches:

> This is a gag rule. It is the worst gag rule that I have seen in the 33 years in which I have served in the Congress. It denies this body the opportunity to perfect a bill which even the sponsors agree requires substantial perfection and improvement.[32]

Bill Frenzel, the ranking Republican on Ways and Means, agreed:

> The rule is odious. Its stench includes stolen jurisdiction, no debate, waivers of regular rules, and the special odor of favoritism. There is only one way to freshen the air. The rule has to be defeated.[33]

30. Rovner, " 'Pepper Bill' Pits Politics Against Process," p. 1492.
31. *Congressional Record*, daily edition (June 8, 1988), p. H4017.
32. Ibid.
33. Ibid., p. H4018.

Rostenkowski eventually closed the debate for the rule's opponents, followed by a brilliant peroration from Pepper, who won the hearts of his colleagues but not their votes. The rule went down to defeat, 169-243, taking Pepper's bill along with it.

Dingell could characterize H. Res. 466 as a "gag rule," but in this case the restrictive nature of the rule was not members' only concern, nor probably even their primary concern. The more contentious issue was whether the text of the Pepper bill should be brought to the floor at all without first having been reported by Energy and Commerce and Ways and Means. By effectively "extracting" his bill from the two committees, Pepper and the other Rules Democrats had intruded on the jurisdiction of two of the House's most influential committee chairmen, a situation all concerned normally strain to avoid. As a result, many Democrats found themselves caught in the middle, and they were not at all happy about it. They would have to choose between offending the two chairmen, whose committees could help or hurt them all, or offending the chairman of Rules, who also happened to be a virtual folk hero to many senior citizens.

Moreover, Democratic members could not look to the Speaker for an unambiguous signal. Several weeks earlier, Wright had seemed to defend Pepper's strategy against Rosenkowski's criticisms.[34] And during the debate, Pepper asserted that "the Committee on Rules never encroaches upon the jurisdiction of any committee of this House except when the Speaker of this House, our distinguished Speaker, specifically approves, as he does this resolution. . . ."[35] Yet Wright himself failed to join the debate, as he sometimes did when he wanted to rally his fellow Democrats on issues important to him. Some Democrats also wondered why their leaders had not taken a whip count to assess support for the bill, as they often do on legislation that they actively support. "Our deal was only to get it to the floor," one of Wright's aides was quoted as saying.[36] In short, Democratic members could wonder how much their Speaker really cared.

There were other factors involved, of course. Many members had serious reservations about how much Pepper's proposal would cost and how well it would work. And they also enjoyed some political "cover." If they voted against the rule, they could defend themselves against political attack by emphasizing the virtues of the other catastrophic health care bill they had just sent to the president for his signature. From the perspective

34. Rovner, "'Pepper Bill' Pits Politics Against Process," p. 1493.
35. *Congressional Record*, daily edition (June 8, 1988), p. H4046.
36. Rovner, "'Pepper Bill' Pits Politics Against Process," p. 1491.

of this study, however, the moral of the Pepper episode is that the Rules Committee remains the servant of the House, not its master. Its power and success depend ultimately on its ability to serve others—by promoting the Speaker's party program, protecting Democratic committee leaders and their bills, and making floor proceedings more manageable for the members at large. In this case, instead, the committee's Democrats failed to receive active and visible support from their party leaders, they provoked opposition from two powerful committee chairmen, and they placed their fellow partisans in a politically awkward and dangerous situation on the floor. And so they lost.

But this episode is instructive precisely because it was so unusual. We began this study by asserting that the Rules Committee stands at the crossroads of the legislative process in the House, where the interests of members, committees, and party leaders can converge or collide. The committee's influence rests not only on its formal powers, but also on its demonstrated ability to weigh and respond to these interests successfully as it balances its partisan and institutional responsibilities. One of the primary reasons for its success in the contemporary House has been its innovative use of an expanding repertoire of procedures by which it has helped the House to adapt to internal changes and respond to external pressures. By arranging the pieces of special rules into acceptable combinations suitable for controversial bills, the committee has added a new dimension to legislative strategy in the House.

The most important of these pieces usually have involved restrictions, in one form or another, on the ability of representatives to propose amendments. What began in the late 1950s as a means for managing the peculiar difficulties of tax bills has evolved into a general strategy of the majority party for managing uncertainty on the House floor. The complexities and unpredictability of postreform House politics have spawned some remarkable efforts by the majority party leadership and the Rules Committee to find new techniques for setting and controlling the floor agenda. The effects of these new techniques have reverberated throughout the House, as members have altered their political calculations and strategies for offering amendments, committees have discovered and capitalized on new sources of protection from attack on the floor, and the minority party has found itself confronted with new constraints on its ability to propose alternatives to majority party policies. In consequence, a new trade of parliamentary craftsmanship has developed in the House, and a new era of decisionmaking has begun.

Index

136